Noble Ways

Lay-bys In My Life

Noble Ways

Lay-bys In My Life

Roy Noble

Published by Accent Press Ltd – 2010

ISBN 9781907016035

Printed and bound in the Malta

Cover design by Red Dot Design

Quotation from *The Collier* by Vernon Watkins reproduced
by kind permission of Mrs Gwen Watkins

DEDICATED TO

Elaine, in love and the certain thought that I could
not function without her.
And to Richard, our Number 1 in all ways, who
now holds the Noble line.

WITH SPECIAL AND GRATEFUL THANKS TO:

Charlotte Evans for the title, Catrin Collier, author and novelist, Phil Carradice, author, and Sophie Thomas, BBC Wales Producer, who drew the short straw and kindly agreed to read this Noble, or ignoble, effort and made invaluable suggestions and observations along many kinks and corners.

My sincere gratitude also to Eleri Jones, ex-BBC producer, who did sterling work on the editing front and added thanks to Natalie James, word processor and typist, who, incredibly, deciphered my scrawl.

PROLOGUE

SHE CAME STRAIGHT FOR me out of the crowd at the Royal Welsh Show. There was no avoiding her, as she looked me in the eye. She was clearly a Romany, a gypsy; I'd met women like her many times selling pegs around the houses.

'Can I read your palm for a pound?' she asked.

Being a rather insecure kind of fellow, I gave her two quid just to make sure.

'I see three things,' she said. 'I don't believe you will win anything, like the football pools or the lottery, but you'll be fine.

'Secondly, I think, in years to come, you'll die near a mountain or a river.'

Now in Wales, you've a fair chance of doing that.

'The third vision I see, is of you having three careers.'

She was a wee bit misty as to what the third career was. A hint would have been handy.

Well, I'm in my sixties so, unless the government wants us to work for ever, the third career had better raise its head sooner rather than later. I wait with bated breath for a clue from the far horizon.

If the third career is, in any way, as fulfilling as the first two, then I'll have no complaints. For my benefit, the Good Lord has always worked a full week. He's never been reduced to short time.

Education and broadcasting have been fertile fields for me and some of the more telling experiences are related in this book but as I still work for the BBC, tales continue to unfold and will be shelved for another time, another place, another book. The spine of this publication draws on early life and the ingredients that made this 'broth of a boy' a Nobleman in Wales, if only by name.

Everyone is born with definite qualities, weaknesses, strengths, abilities and ineptitudes. It's life that hones the original product and I firmly believe that each of us is sculpted by two influences, people and places. Our forebears have moulded us and, in turn, as we get older, we become the sculptors, influencing and shaping those who follow.

Never have thoughts that your children or your grandchildren lack respect or never listen to a word you say. Thirty years down the trail, they will be saying and doing things because they saw you do them and say them. You will "go on", be reassured.

My early moulding was in Brynaman and my story takes in the people and places that shaped me. The village, the infants and junior school, all left their mark upon me, thankfully never a scar.

The grammar school at Ammanford in my formative years threw me headlong towards College in Cardiff, and then to a map of teaching lay-bys and life's stopovers.

Aberdare became my home, by lust and love,

and I've been well content in the Heads of the Valleys for over 40 years. I had the better deal on the relationship front, for Elaine is very attractive and must have first met me on a dark or stormy night when she was totally disorientated.

Richard is our only child. I think we would have liked more but it wasn't to be. My wife Elaine is one of three, her mother was one of three and her sister had three, so three was a figure that came to mind for ourselves. Number one in each of those trios was a girl so, psychologically, we must have been expecting a girl. In fact, when Richard was born, I had been sent to another room, because of complications, it was that era, and when they informed me that we had a fine son, my response was, "Are you sure it's a boy?" The reply was succinct, "Mr Noble. I've been in midwifery for thirty years so I'm pretty positive about this one … he's a boy!" When a nurse handed me our brand new Noble it was magical and I can still feel his weight and warmth to this day.

I was an only child, so the Noble re-production number was what prevailed on the conveyor belt in our house. Richard is Number 1 son, and we're proud of him.

The move from education to broadcasting was a chasm-covering leap. After all, I had a good job; I was a primary school headmaster. In the end, fate took a hand, and my intellect was brought into question, as will be revealed, an insult turned to incentive.

They say the world can be divided into two

kinds of people, those who "do" and those who get the credit for it. I think the world can be divided into three kinds of people, those who "make things happen" those who "watch things happen" and, those who merely ask, "What's happening then?"

I've never been a decisive person. If I was an army general we'd still be on some hill debating where the attack should be. I believe though, that fate can help.

It was once suggested that "fate is what happens to you and destiny is what you do with what happens to you", but, now and again, you have to put your head above the parapet, so that destiny can see you.

Well, at vital moments of my life, I was pushed by some hidden force, director or angel, so I have been fortunate in my life-support team.

Everyone has the right to be the hero in their own novel, even if others believe it to be only a booklet, or even a pamphlet.

Everyone has a right to make his mark, a sign to show "I was here!"

None of the experiences, stories or events unfolded here are heroic, but it is a Noble tale, honestly remembered and related.

Each tale has its place and, in the list of communities listed in the book, something happened there that moved it in my mind, to a memory beyond its mere geographical spot in Wales.

If society is a quilt, then I place my little patch before you in a free-range, random design. In my mind, you cannot have the foresight to know where

4

you're going without having the insight of knowing where you are and the hindsight of where you've been and what brought you here.

For the Nobleman in Wales, it's a journey "Back to the Future".

A MATTER OF PEDIGREE

I WAS ONCE TOLD that if you know where your great-great-grandmother, on your mother's side, was from, then that's your true ancestral patch on the planet.

I don't know if that has a grain of truth in it, probably not, bearing in mind most family backgrounds are not so much "trees", but thick shrubberies, or complex bushes. On the other hand, if it is so, then I am from the depths of Carmarthenshire, around Caio, Pumsaint and Crugybar, near the famed Roman goldmines of Dolau Cothi. The ancient sinews of that rural patch puts a pedigree Welsh stamp on my credentials. Beyond that relative certainty, it all gets a bit elastic.

What of the rest of me? Now, we're talking a cocktail of bloodlines. Going backwards on my father's side on the Noble trail, I can take in Penybanc, Ammanford, with a touch of British Columbia, Canada, thrown in, Pembroke Dock, Tenby over three generations, Tor Point in Cornwall and south of Bury St Edmunds in Suffolk.

Add to all of that the fact the man I thought was my grandfather on my mother's side, wasn't, and my great-grandfather on the same side is also lost in the mists of time, a total unknown to me, and you can see that my lineage doesn't get back to the time of the Mabinogion legends without several side-steps.

So, when you say you're Welsh, what are you? Well, I've been both suspicious and jealous of those who say, with authority, that they can trace their family tree back to Maxen Wledig, or Taliesin or Mardwyddan, the son of Llyr around about 500 BC, when the White Book of Rhydderch and the Red Book of Hergest had their ancient stories incorporated into the Mabinogion, the mythology of Wales. I couldn't get far on that pure, ancient road, without falling in the gutter several times.

To have deep roots, and a real sense of place and belonging, is one thing, but I do get a little uncomfortable as to how near the hearth and fire of home many of us would be allowed to curl, if scrutiny of background and genealogy was too stringent. Research on the family tree is a dicey business, with frail branches, twirly twigs and nasty knots at every level.

The Celts, so we're told, came to Cymru in stages, from the Halstadt region of what is now southern Germany, or north from Spain and the Iberian Peninsular; the former being tall and blond, the latter being dark-haired and stocky, with legs that were short but very willing. I think there's a strong case for a lot more of our ancestral tribes having come from Iberia than Germany, for the retail store Marks and Spencer will tell you that the typical Welsh Celt, of South Wales in particular, has an inside leg measurement of 29 inches. More 29 inches inside leg trousers are sold in South

Wales than any other part of Britain. That's scientific proof enough for me of the Iberian Celtic link.

To all the broth and cawl of personal background must be added other ingredients. There are the "comers in" at various stages of history, especially to the great magnet of the industrial revolution. They arrived from all over the place, the rural areas of Wales, the West Country of England, the Midlands, Ireland, Spain, Italy, Poland and several other countries in Eastern Europe. Wales was a catalyst of industrial advancement and was a melting pot of nationalities, a Klondike on the edge of Western Europe. What a mixture of cultures and ethnic diversity.

My wife Elaine's family, on her mother's side, is from the Cannington area of Somerset. I have a sizeable sliver of Suffolk in me. I'm also told that the Nobles originally came to Britain with the Normans, but there were two types of Noblemen. First, you had the Noble Norman Lord, on horseback, with his helmet, shield and sword to head and hand. Secondly, you had the Noble's men, who held the lord's horse and cleaned up after him. You do not need to guess which Nobles we were, yes, the fellow travellers, the serfs. We knew our place.

All of this makes us mongrels I suppose, but, then again, I've always had a lot of time for mongrels. They're very loyal and tend to be clean around the house.

The pre-Roman tribes who lived in our neck of

the woods and hills had their particular traits and peculiarities, I'm sure, although a common habit was the blue woad decoration on wild Friday nights when they were gate-crashing some Roman "do" or other.

Talking of tribes and their descendants, it was once suggested to me by a Cornishman, when I was filming the Celtic corners of Europe for BBC Wales, that there was more in common between the Cornish Celt and the South Wales Celts than there was between the South Walians and the North Walians. It's an interesting theory but with devolution in Wales and the Welsh Assembly Government seeking new powers, it's probably best to leave such a suggestion in the "noted, but no action envisaged" file, at the back of the cupboard. It would only cause tears and a gnashing of politically sensitive teeth.

Other countries must have the same problem when defining nationality. Take the English now, there's a deep dusting of hundreds and thousands on their national trifle.

I think the English, as a nation, are much maligned. After all, if the Welsh have trouble defining Welshness, the English have a problem with Englishness, hundreds of times over.

Who are the English? It's a big, big question. I once tackled this query with a Welshman who has strong xenophobic feelings about the English, particularly on rugby international days.

'I hate them!' he'd say.

'Which English are you talking about, Cedric?' I'd ask. 'What about Lancashire, Yorkshire, and the

North of England generally?'

'No, they're all right, they are,' he'd reply. 'Salt of the earth, working-class, like us!'

'How about the Midlands then?'

'No, they're fine, they've got the same problems we have, definitely feet-on-the- ground people!'

'West Country then?'

'No, a lot of them are Celts like us.'

'Well, we're narrowing the field down now, Cedric, what about the south-east, Surrey perhaps?'

'They're the ones, they're the snobs, not the ones in *Eastenders* on TV mind, those others, the gentry toffs!'

'I tell you what, Cedric,' says I, 'I know a lot of Welsh people who are doing very well in Surrey, mind.'

On the other side of the coin, it's not an easy question to ask what the English truly feel about the Welsh. No blanket response, I'm sure. Different views from different experiences with long-held, many-hued images from contacts that confirm, or deny, imagined stereotypes.

It's the perception, isn't it, of how others see us. Some will have stereotypes in their brains that muddle their minds and manners. Some of us in Wales have the same problem as we look east at our English neighbours. One or two let us down badly, as was the case in Westgate Street, Cardiff, on the morning of the Wales v. England rugby international in 2009. Two yobs in Welsh colours burnt the flag of St George. Now, I wonder what the reaction would have been had the Welsh

Read "Neighbours from Hell?" by Mike Parker.

Dragon flag been burnt outside Twickenham before a game? I suspect a report to the Race Relations Board.

Now come on, we've matured beyond this behaviour. Control over Wales by England after the Act of Union in 1536 has left many a justifiable grievance and itchy sore over centuries, but we've moved on, we're re-emerging. Wales is now developing and widening its shoulders as a nation and it needs to do so with a dignity and growing authority that attracts respect from the family of nations.

I also have a distinct leaning towards the sanctity of the individual. We are what we are, we're from where we're from and we are unique. I believe everyone has a right to be and to be made to feel of value. Of course, in society, with equal rights should come equal responsibilities, and some people need to be stringently reminded of that on occasion but, given respect, dignity and encouragement, everyone has a contribution to make. Or is that too sanitized and naive a view? Good Lord, I hope not.

I have had the good fortune to have travelled widely, and, to be honest; most people are the same everywhere, genuine, friendly and reasonable. I'm an "internationalist" on that score. Get to a strata of society below the politicians, get to the real people and, in most cases, you won't be disappointed. They have the same fears, hopes, despairs and aspirations as the rest of us.

It's good to build bridges too. On many expeditions, I've travelled to join Welsh Societies abroad, usually for St David's Day, and it's good to report that 99.9% of the Welsh I've met in other lands fly our flag superbly well. They are great ambassadors and image painters as to what the "real" Welsh are like.

Mind you, the other 0.1% should have been stopped at Chepstow or Mold, just to avoid embarrassment. There's always one, isn't there? To be fair, that's true of all nations I suppose.

I have in mind that Brian Harris quote from his poem "In passing", that you often see on plaques in craft shops around Wales:

To be born Welsh is to be privileged,
Not with a silver spoon in your mouth,
But music in your heart
And poetry in your soul.

I could add "And with strength in your sinews and with power in your blood", but the expectation of others might be too much – after all; you can't do it all, can you? Anyway, if you look at the back of some of those plaques, it says "Made in China".

TENBY IN MY SOUL

IN THE COLD LIGHT of day, I suppose it would have been classified as stealing from Woolworth. I was only seven at the time. I was under some stress and pressure and, after all, in my book it was only a replacement, but their "end of week" balances would have been out, and their executives would have wondered about the broken yellow plastic dog with red ears.

Tenby was an annual holiday jaunt in those days. I would go down and see Grandpa and Grandma in Tenby. They lived in No. 8 Trafalgar Road, just next door to the barbershop. They were my grandparents on my father's side and they were very much, in Pembrokeshire terms, "down below" people, with their strong South Pembrokeshire accent. I looked forward to our week in Tenby every year.

We'd go on the South Wales Transport bus from Brynaman to Gwaun Cae Gurwen, or GCG, then on to Carmarthen on a Western Welsh bus. There, we'd change buses again, to Epsworth's, for the final leg of our journey to the sea. As we were, invariably, the first in the queue at Carmarthen, we got the front seats upstairs, and I'd have the chance to stand all the way, grabbing the rail to seek out that first view of the sea. From the top of a double-decker bus, it came just after Red Roses and Llanteg when Caldey Island heaved into view on the far horizon … exciting beyond!

My grandpa, Jimmy Noble, was a genial, lovely man, with a big moustache, turned yellow in parts by his heavy smoking, a flat Dai cap and, as often as not, wearing a waistcoat, even in warm weather on the beach. He was a painter by profession, not an artist, but a painter of houses, being a specialist in "graining", using a comb to run through the paint to create a flowing design. Their front door at No. 8 Trafalgar Road was magnificent and one of my regrets is that, in later life, I didn't buy the door. By the time I decided to purchase it, the new owners had painted it blue.

I did have some compensation some time later, from Tenby Golf Club. At a speaking engagement they presented me with a model of the door properly grained and on a plinth. I still have it.

No. 8 Trafalgar Road was an exciting place, with an indoor toilet, a large sailing yacht on top of a cupboard in the bathroom, and a parlour that had a sideboard full of silver cups, won by Grandpa's yachts. Actually, Grandpa had two full-size yachts, the *Doric* and the *Elsie*, in the harbour at Tenby. They were sailing dinghies really, but, to me, they were yachts. They were manned for him by a couple of men in the town, Val and Little Jimmy and, they would race in various competitions and regattas, as well as taking them out for mackerel fishing, as needs arose. Grandpa also had a proper pair of binoculars, powerful and heavy, the first pair I'd ever seen, let alone handled. With those binoculars I was very often doing duties as a navy destroyer or submarine captain. From Castle Hill, you could see for ever.

I never once sailed in the *Elsie*. I was a *Doric* man. Dad and I would often go out fishing for mackerel with Little Jimmy, who had a hump on his back. As I recall, not one of us wore a life jacket, there was no "Health and Safety" then. In fact, in a photograph I have at home, I'm seen holding up a small catch of fish, dressed sedately in a non-marine gabardine Mac. And wearing a school cap.

I was a little afraid of my grandmother. Grandma Noble was always dressed in black; she had a slight limp and used a stick. Her hair was tied closely together in a bun with a parting down the middle. She was strict. She didn't take prisoners. I remember one wet day, Mam and I were in the parlour looking at the cups on the sideboard and, we could hear her, slowly coming down the stairs, two feet and a stick, in a rhythm that gives a clue that this is no messenger of good news. The clonk of the stick opened the parlour door; in she came, holding in her hand something that looked like wet paper.

'You'd better talk to him,' she said to my mother. 'When he goes to the toilet, he's using too much toilet paper. It's a waste, train him better.'

It's odd what children keep in their minds for ever, because that was a traumatic moment for me. I've never forgotten it. I thought the message was given too bluntly, too unkindly, without any awareness of the sensitivity of my mother or myself, but, from that moment on in life, I've always been very frugal with toilet paper. You see, toilet paper was a new experience for me. Toilet paper probably came to Tenby, being a tourist area, a couple of years before Brynaman. Our toilet paper in the toilet out the back was the Daily Herald, hanging on the nail, cut into squares if you wanted to be "posh" about it. Grandma Noble probably didn't think it through, so she never realised that, in my toilet training, she left a scar in my mind about those personal, private, contemplative, "kharzi" moments.

Tenby was a place of adventure for a young boy. It had nooks, crannies, alleys, paths and steps that took you down to the harbour, to the beaches and caves, to the lifeboat station, and on to take in the views of Caldey Island in the south and of Coskar Rock and Monkstone Point in the north.

Oddly enough, many years later, I was told that the Merchant's House in Tenby, the oldest house there I believe, was where the Nobles first lived when they came to the town as coastguards. It was then a tenement building, so several families lived there, but it was nice to have it pin-pointed as a previous Noble home. Another Noble abode was the house in the Parade, near the Fire Station, which has a sad family history. Four of my grandfather's siblings died there of typhoid, during their teenage years or early twenties, when the water supply was contaminated.

Overlooking the North Beach, with magnificent views over Carmarthen Bay, is the Royal Gatehouse Hotel. It was recently severely affected by fire, but in the early 1950s it was *the* place to stay in Tenby.

OH LORD WHAT A MORNING

Many years later, after I had been in broadcasting a short while, I was given the great honour of being invited to be President of the Tenby Male Choir. I have happily been in that position ever since. It's always a very, very pleasant occasion when we go down to see them perform, or join them for their annual Christmas lunch, which is in January by the way. That must be something to do with the Pembrokeshire pace of life. There is such a thing as "The Pembrokeshire Promise" I'm told, whereby, if you ask for something to be done, by craftsmen for instance, it will always be soon … "it's a promise" … meaning eventually.

There's also the "Pembrokeshire Trap". The fact that the County 'draws' you in and captivates you with its attractions, beauty and pace of life. I know many people who have taken jobs or professional posts in Pembrokeshire in the belief that it will be good for their CV and career development. In their mind they saw such moves as short-term or a good stepping-stone, but in all cases, in my experience, they became enticed and enamoured by the County and never leave.

With regard to the Tenby Choir, the event I will always remember was when Elaine, Richard and I were invited to join them on a tour to Romania. The BBC agreed that while there I could do some recordings. Romania at the time was a Communist regime and all visitors were regarded as suspicious. Elaine and I had been undermined somewhat, by a gentleman from BBC World Service in London who was a Romanian, and wanted us to take some packages into the country.

'Someone will meet you at the airport or come to your hotel,' he said.

Add this disquieting approach to the fact that Elaine was a fearful flier and you can see that we were not having the best of possible preparations for the trip.

On the day we were due to leave Cardiff Airport, this tired Yllussion aircraft came in from Taron Airlines of Romania. A big woman disembarked, dressed in a leather trench coat. She introduced herself as "Head of Security" and came up to me.

'You are the Presidente, are you not?'

I nodded at this vision from a James Bond film. Clearly she was not sufficiently high in the Communist Party to have access to a dentist.

'You and your wife will sit in the VIP lounge in the back of the plane.'

Elaine, a fully paid-up member of the 'Fearful Fliers Society', found the back of the plane back doubly claustrophobic and was so tense and traumatized that she refused to sit down. She burst into tears, sobbing.

'I want to get off.'

There was no consoling her, so we got off, Richard, Elaine and myself.

The big woman in the trench coat glared and hissed. 'If you are getting off the plane, then your cases must come off too.'

She quickly organized the pilot, a baggage handler from Cardiff Airport and myself into a chain gang, while the hold of the aircraft was searched, the cases found and passed along the line. As the well-known hymn says, "Oh, Lord, what a morning!"

Sian Evans of the BBC had arranged to travel with us, for BBC recording purposes, so she remained on the plane and on the trip. Romania, as a country, in those days, was a hard Communist regime. When Sian reported back on her return, she declared that a lot of her tapes had been stolen while she was away from her hotel room. The Romanian tour guide would only talk freely to everyone when he was outside any building or, better still, on a mountain.

The choir stayed in the Carpathian Mountains for a few days, in a very prestigious hotel. However, one day the hotel had no water, so they visited the local water engineer and bribed him to turn off the village water supply and put the hotel supply back on. Cars with "even numbers" on their registration plates, were allowed on the road one Sunday, and those with "odd numbers" on the following Sunday. Such was the petrol shortage.

BUDDING KLEPTOMANIAC

So to the last memory, the one I mentioned at the head of this chapter. Perhaps I've been putting off the notorious Woolworth incident. When we were on holiday, my mother usually spent some of the week buying presents for my cousins back home in

Brynaman. For cousin John she'd bought a small, yellow plastic dog, with a convincing bark, if you pushed his backside. He had red ears. I can see him now. On a rainy day I was in the parlour, killing time, when I started playing with the toy canine and one of his ears came off in my hand. I didn't know what to do. I was desperate and I had a mind's vision and a fair inclination as to my mother's reaction. After all, money was tight in those days, so I decided on a bold plan of action. I would take the plastic dog back to Woolworth and change it for another.

I walked into the Tenby Woolworth store, found the counter where the dog had been bought and, my luck was in, there were still some for sale. I nervously looked around, found the coast clear, placed the broken dog on the counter and took an unblemished replacement – and walked out.

I am pleased now that I have shared that memory with you, because it has been weighing heavily upon my shoulders and my mind for years and years and years. That unsolved crime can now be scrubbed off the Dyfed Powys police records. Sadly there's no recompense for Woolworth because all their stores have closed. How I did it, I don't know. Why I did it, I do know. Even now, when I lie in bed, unable to sleep, that incident creeps back into my mind, and the hair stands up on the back of my head.

In the cold light of day, I suppose it would have been classified as stealing from Woolworth. I was only seven at the time. I was under some stress and pressure and, after all, in my book, it was only a replacement, but their "end of week" balances would have been out, and their executives would have wondered about the broken yellow plastic dog with red ears.

GOING UP THE MOUNTAIN

HE ALWAYS HAD THE same habit when he was feeling low. He'd take a knife from the cutlery drawer, open the back door and systematically sharpen the knife, back and forth, back and forth, across the doorstep. Then, tightening his coat about him, he'd put the knife in his pocket and say, 'I'm going up the mountain.'

My grandmother would sit quietly in the corner of the kitchen next to the fire, saying nothing, but crying quietly to herself. It was always like this whenever my grandfather's spirits were low and the obvious depression was upon him. I was just a little boy and didn't understand that he was a man of moods. I saw him enact that doorstep scene only twice, but the images went deep, to become real and permanent.

He'd never go far "up the mountain". Never far enough to get lost and, if there was a low mountain mist, he'd never step too far away from the Llangadog Road because there was an added risk in taking that extra stride, off into the wet peat of the wild moorland.

My father, who worked nights, would go after him, losing a shift of work in doing so. He'd always find him easily, even if the mist were down. When he'd found him and turned to bring him home, or so my father said, my grandfather would always say, 'OK, let go of my arm now, in case some of the boys coming out of the Black Mountain Inn see us.'

Funny, Francis Lewis, my grandfather, was always kind to me but he had this black side to his character that now colours my memory of him. It's strange to think that, years later; I was to find out that he wasn't my grandfather at all. My grandmother married him some years after my mother was born. Although I've tried to find out who my real grandfather was, I've always hit a brick wall in my investigations. I never asked my mother and my grandmother was long passed away before genealogy and "family trees" became fashionable, so I didn't get the chance to gently enquire of her.

I loved my grandmother, she used to take my side if my mother was fraught at any time, like the time I managed to lock myself in the pantry. As a little one, I could never say Mamgu, I could only manage "Gu", so, all my life "Gu" she remained. She was a small, wiry woman and my mother was of different build and facial features, again raising the question as to who her errant father might have been.

We lived near the Black Mountain, just two hundred yards if you went past the farm, so it became my adventure playground. Although I've lived happily in Aberdare, for over forty years, the Black Mountain of Brynaman is my spiritual home; it is in my psyche and my soul. It was there that the formative years moulded the man.

As a boy the moorland there offered just

23

enough flat patches to play rugby, soccer and cricket. The River Garw held the upper and lower black pools, Pwll Du Uchaf and Pwll Du Isaf, for swimming in gangs. To the west was Wimberry Mountain, a place to take care, to beware, a place never to visit on your own, because children got kidnapped there, or so my mother said.

Much higher up the mountain slope was Nant Caws, Cheese Stream, that came tumbling down from the peat lake. Beyond the Derlwyn Turn on the Llangadog road was the long hike up to Garreg Lwyd, the grey stone cairn on the very summit of the Black Mountain where the views took in, to the south, Swansea Bay; the smoke of Port Talbot; Somerset and, if you stood on tippy-toes, I'm sure that was the northern coast of Africa. Northwards, the vista stretched over beautiful fields and rolling hills, onwards to Snowdonia and, was that Scotland in the far-off summer haze? When you're a boy, you can see that far.

Garreg Lwyd, and the western reaches of the Brecon Beacons, was a full day's march and required an old army haversack holding a bottle of water, or Dandelion and Burdock pop, condensed milk sandwiches and an apple. It was on such a day that Berian Evans and I met a man who suddenly popped up from behind a boulder. After a brief chat, he disappeared, just as suddenly as he came and, although we stared after him towards the distant slopes leading, steeply, down to Llyn y Fan Fach, the home of the "Lady of the Lake" and her legendary tale, we could see no trace of him. Had he been real; this sudden, solid apparition who had chanced upon us, or the ghost of a fell walker from another time and another place? That mountain and moorland has a link with the ancients, so nothing is beyond the pale and everything is possible. Berian and I decided he was a spectre, so we quickly packed up our haversack and hurried away from "Brigadoon".

Where was our mind, on another hiking day, when we accepted an invitation from a roving Aberystwyth University lecturer, to join him in potholing down limestone sink-holes? We crawled through passages where our chins touched the floor and the tops of our heads scraped the roof. Crazy stuff, we had three torches but he had the only helmet. The Black Mountain was our, close to hand, Himalayas, the Sahara Desert and wide prairies, we could explore them all up there.

An annual adventure was the Whit Monday walk to Carreg Cennen Castle. Children aged ten to thirteen would heed the pilgrimage to Carreg Cennen. I don't know why. Perhaps the reason went back to the eons of time and oral history had a cough; missing out the tale when next it was passed on at the tribal campfire. Children from Garnant, Brynaman, Glanaman, Ammanford, Llandybie and all points of the Amman Valley answered the call.

From Brynaman, we headed over the western stretch of Black Mountain. Using the three ancient Cairns as markers. Once there, the day had a pattern, down to the Cennen River, up to the castle, a picnic of strawberry or condensed milk, sandwiches and bottles of water, then down to the dungeon for fun and frolics, then off home.

An extra adventure was added one year when Tecwyn Thomas, John Salter and myself left it late to leave the castle. By the time we reached the mountain crest following the Llangadog road, keeping away from the peat bog; mist and darkness had descended.

We tried thumbing a lift but there weren't many cars about in those days. I think there were only about half a dozen vehicles in Brynaman, and the undertaker owned three of those. God, however, was not working a "three day week" on that Bank Holiday. Suddenly, on the crest of the ridge, through the swirling mist and growing darkness, there it was, unmistakable – the shape of a parked car.

The occupants were a courting couple and you can imagine them quietly, privately, canoodling in a cwtch, when out of the darkness, three waifs came running towards their car and start banging on the window. It must have taken years off their lives.

Fair play, they gave us a lift. Good job too, my mother had already told the local police that we were lost on the mountain. That courting couple were heroes – and to keep things tidy, they married soon afterwards.

SONG OF THE EARTH

Many years later, I found myself, again as one of a trio, alongside the road that led to Carreg Cennen Castle. It was a summer of rare drought in

Brynaman and the villagers of Mountain Road re-found themselves again, in sharing water from a spring on the hill because the council was rationing water supply.

With me on that road was Berian Evans, violinist and now viola player in Perth, Australia and Delme Bryn Jones; a renowned opera singer of international fame, who was known locally as Boyo Sienkin. He had reached success on the old traditional, impeccable, path to stardom, having worked for a short while in coal-mines, winning a Welsh international rugby cap at youth level as a prop forward and stepping up the singing ladder via eisteddfodau. He was the son of the cobbler on Station Road; a man of intellect and long conversation if you were waiting to have your shoes done.

Delme was married at the time to a German lady, or so I believe, and he was with us on the mountain trying to wash his German Wartburg car in a very shallow pool of water. Berian and I helped as best we could, given the drought; each small bucket of water had to travel far along the car panels, as Delme regaled us with his experiences in the opera houses of the world, while still re-affirming his roots and the fact that the Black Mountain was his spiritual home. For all the happiness I've enjoyed in the Cynon Valley and "Sweet Aberdare" it's mine too.

CRAIG Y LLYN CALLING

Much later in my life the hills, mountains and

moorlands of Wales continued to be a magnet – a calling. Sometimes the calling was general in its invitation, sometimes more specific. I still answer one extra special beckoning around about Christmas time and the call has to be fulfilled by Twelfth Night if my New Year is to start properly.

The duty takes me along the Hirwaun to Treherbert Road, climbing up to the northern ridge of the old South Wales Coalfield, to a spot near Craig y Llyn, the ancient ice-age lake, and there I drink whisky with a friend.

He died some years ago and his ashes were scattered there, on the moorland ridge between the Cynon and Rhondda Valleys. Every year I spend time with him, as I did weekly, in the latter years of his life.

Rhydwen Williams was a minister of religion by profession but so much more by inclination and interest. A renowned writer and poet, winning two Crowns in the National Eisteddfod of Wales, he was also a "bon vivant", an expansive character, well able to understand and sympathise with the frailties of man. Indeed, he once told me he had trouble with two of the Ten Commandments himself but felt that a mark of eight out of ten wasn't too bad in any exam.

His rich, deep voice had a disarming, enchanting quality and was particularly effective in weakening any woman within a fifty-yard radius. His literary prowess extended from his beloved Welsh language into English, in his later years, moving him to social association, and then friendship, with Richard Burton and Elizabeth

Taylor. In writing scripts for the Granada-produced television soap, *Coronation Street*, he swore to me that, at its origin, they wanted to call it "Florizel Street", but it was he who came up with the now universally famous name.

I'm tempted to believe him. He was incorrigible, caring little for money, whether it was due in or out. When writing for Granada, he was often "double booked" and parishioners who were expecting him at a chapel service, would, on such occasions, have to make do with a tape recorder in the pulpit, playing one of his sermons.

I met him weekly for a chinwag and some lubrication of the vocal chords. His world, after suffering a stroke, was a small study-bedroom behind the kitchen in his terraced house in Trecynon. Underneath the bed, he had two bottles, one for his natural needs, the other Famous Grouse whisky, which he hid behind his slippers lest Margaret, his wife, found it. It was a game they played, for Margaret knew full well what was going on. After all, on retreat from his bedroom, it wasn't the smell of Darjeeling or Assam tea on my breath.

After his passing, my weekly visits became annual pilgrimages, up to the high moorland ridge near Craig y Llyn, where Rhydwen now embraces the elements. It is a wild place, steeped in a history that comes unbroken from the Bronze Age and allows the soul to wander and wonder in sacred solitude.

Looking north from the ridge you can view the site of Tower Colliery, famous for its gesture of defiance against an erstwhile and errant government. You can also see the expanse of Hirwaun Common on which, it is said, the first red flag of dissent and intent, in the entire world, was flown.

Fittingly, it was also suggested to me that, if you could travel east on the latitude that scythes through the Craig y Llyn ridge, the next highest land that you would come upon is in the Urals of Russia. I'd love to prove that one day.

As you drop down towards the Rhondda Fawr, heading for the villages of Treherbert and Blaenrhondda below the dramatic, flat-topped ridge of Blaen Pych, which would not look out of place in a Western film, there is a car park on the left near the forestry plantations. It is there that Rhydwen and I now share our annual drink, musing on our memories. I don't know if the spot is sacred, touched by an ancient lore, or, perhaps, near a portal to a parallel universe but, when the mist is down and heavy, interesting and pondering happenings can occur.

Just a couple of Christmases ago as I sat in my car, raised a glass to Rhydwen and wondered about the two empty cars parked nearby, I saw a man walking his dog through the damp mist. He kept coming into view, then out of view again, repeatedly leading his dog in and out of the mist and the adjacent pine forest. Soon, another car pulled in, driven by a lady. The man, immediately, took his dog back to his own car, scuttled it into the back seat and, joining the lady, went "walkies" into the mist and forest.

They had only just disappeared when out of the low cloud, a large American stretch limousine turned up. It stopped alongside my car, eight Japanese gentlemen got out, posed for a misty photograph and, two clicks later, they were gone.

I watched the limousine's rear fog lights disappear and, became aware of a lone figure, slowly climbing up the grassy slope. His gait was marked and it soon became clear that he had only one leg and was walking with the aid of a crutch. He looked like someone out of an historical novel and I looked around for other, possible, "cast" members. He made his way to the other unattended car, threw his crutch in, swung into the driving seat and, quite quickly, set off.

All these minor incidents took place within the span of fifteen minutes. The dog was still in the other car and the assignation in the woods, if that was what it was, obviously continued, well hidden by the secret, concealing, heavy mist.

To my mind, the spot where Rhydwen's ashes are spread is a place of pilgrimage, measured and tended by time. It is mystical, possibly magical, but certainly melancholy in its air and sense of those who once "passed this way". Could it be that such a place invites "incidents"? Is it near a portal to another dimension … or was the whisky a more potent quality and strength that day?

I'm sure Rhydwen knows.

Mountains and moorlands are sizable measures of "What is Wales?" They are more than just geology, geography and physical features of terrain. They mould the fabric of who and what you are and, where you're truly from. Like the sea, they're indelible in their effect and influence, keeping their secrets and stories across the ages, encompassing you in their unending, unfolding saga. For each and every one of us, it is a personal relationship.

Walking through my memory, whenever I think of "the wild moorland play area", the adventures of boyhood bring warm smiles of recollection. It was on the Black Mountain that I played; where I hiked and where my adventures unfolded. It was there, on its slopes leading to Carreg Cennen Castle, that I did my courting, and it was there, alone and bereft, that I did my crying, when my father and mother, in turn, passed away. It is a place where elements and emotions become one.

That image of my grandfather, or the man I thought was my grandfather, sharpening his knife on the doorstep, his coat held closely about him, saying those forbidding words, 'I'm going up the mountain', is an abiding one.

Thankfully, it's just the one memory; the single dark patch on my "mountain quilt" of many colours. Most are bright, sunny, and smile-inducing in their recall.

HISTORICAL WINDSOR CAFÉ, NOT CASTLE

THE WINDSOR CAFÉ WAS always the first port of call in Swansea. With four men in the house and constant cooking, any café was a lay-by of leisure for my mother, but the Windsor was special.

You see, the Windsor didn't serve mere cups of tea, it turned out pots of tea; silver pots at that. And with your fish and chips, there was always a plate of bread and butter on the side. I was eating chip butties before that name became common.

Everything was served by proper waitresses in black and white uniforms, and we always had extra chips because one of the waitresses fancied my Uncle Thomas.

I loved the Windsor café except, perhaps, for two things. If there was a queue, I hated sharing a table. It stilted conversation. And, secondly, my mother was always fancying what other people had ordered.

'I wish I'd had the faggots and peas now, they look nice,' was a frequent café comment from Mam, especially if she'd ordered fish.

I remember in my later teenage years, pushing the boat out while courting Elaine, and eating in the

Central Café, Ammanford. We went upstairs where there were linen tablecloths, downstairs being left to the wipe-over gingham designed plastic variety. We had steak and chips for seven shillings and sixpence, only in the Amman Valley it was always "steek and chips", with the emphasis on the double "e" sound in steek.

I recall staring up at the restaurant windows in the Royal Gatehouse Hotel in Tenby when I was on holiday there with my parents, wondering just who those people were who could afford to eat there. Being six feet down, at pavement level, underlined "knowing my place".

As a boy, my only real experience of café culture was being allowed to eat our own sandwiches in the backroom of a Barry Island café, as long as we bought their tea. Those who bought a meal there could sit in the front room, near the windows and take in the views of the fairgrounds and the "what the butler saw" photograph penny slot machines near the beach.

I suppose restaurant habits gradually hit our sensibilities when the Indians and Chinese came to open their late night victuals venues, after pub "stop tap" at 10.30 p.m. Then again, the pubs did fight back with their "chicken in the basket" culinary delights, followed by "scampi in the basket" by the more experimentally adventure-some landlords. Orders had to be at the bar by nine o'clock or you'd be resigned to crisps, pork scratchings or cockles in a jar.

But it has to be said that it is the Windsor Café Swansea that reigns supreme on my taste bud memories.

Swansea was "Mecca" for those of us who lived in the western Glamorgan and eastern Carmarthenshire valleys. From Brynaman, it was always on the half past nine bus. The South Wales Transport, Brynaman, terminus was the Derlwyn Arms. It's a wonder to me the pub cellar never caved in, with the number of buses that parked above it over the years.

There were six buses a day and if, en-route, one got ahead of schedule, it took a prolonged stop at Clydach Square in the Swansea Valley, next to the cemetery where grass never grew. The smoke from the Mond Nickel Works had seen off all the vegetation some years before.

The itinerary in the sea town was, Windsor Café, the shops, especially Lewis Lewis in the High Street, the department store with the aerial shuttle bucket and wire pay and charge system, and, finally, Swansea Market for laver bread and cockles. If time permitted there was the indulgence of a ride on the Mumbles Railway, with an ice cream near the Bay stop, where the big steel bridge arched the road to reach the beach.

So, eating out was a generally unknown concept when I was a boy, except of course, for Mam's periodic march to the Windsor. It's still there, the Windsor Café, but the excitement of the anticipation, while riding the half past nine South Wales Transport Double-decker from Brynaman, has waned somewhat. Driving an Audi to the Marina bistros, for all their sophistication, doesn't quite hit the same telling, taste filled temptations.

COAL

"DIAMONDS ARE CHUNKS OF coal that hang on in there under pressure."

Or so someone once said.

Well, in the South Wales Valleys, coal was the local diamond, especially when it was dropped by the ton, outside a miner's terraced house and carted to the shed around the back by bucket or wheelbarrow, depending on whether the route was through the house or around it. Miners, and their wives in many cases, could not only tell which coalmine it had come from, but also which seam. Coal was an alternative and additional economy, in that coal miners were given concessionary coal as part of their wage agreement. Eight tons a year was the norm.

As a miner you were not allowed to give away any part of your coal allocation, even as an act of charity. If you were caught at it and reported, you were fined a ton or two and this could leave you short over the year. On the cold of a wintry February night, however, there were many clandestine manoeuvres, when coal was secretly taken to widows or needy families down the road. Some miners hoarded it carefully, one man in our road having two sheds full of coal, one shed as a reserve. It had been a reserve so long, there was ivy growing on the coal.

The coal culture had its own art form. Just as men were proud of their skill in packing the coal in the shed, big lumps to the front to build a wall, with smaller lumps being used to fill in behind the barricade, so the women were just as adept in building and starting a fire in the grate. Once the fire started, a metal blower was put up against the grate so the fire would "draw". A sheet of newspaper covered any gap on the edge of the blower and you knew for certain that the fire was drawing well when the paper started turning brown or black. The newspaper bursting into flame was a step too far. In our area, a good way of building the fire up so that it lasted the night was to mix riddled small coal, or anthracite dust, with clay or cement to form balls called "pele". A layer of those on the fire dampened down the intensity so that you didn't have to start afresh in the morning.

This was especially handy on Sunday mornings because all the cooking, including Sunday dinner, was done by the coal fire, either in heating the oven or providing the platform for all the saucepans. Toast made with a slice of bread on a long fork up against the fire was the finest toast ever. No electric toaster has ever matched it. A particular delicacy was "cheese in the oven". Slices of cheese were placed on a plate, sometimes with flakes of onion, and allowed to bake in the oven. Bliss, with bread and butter. Neither calories nor cholesterol had been invented then. They were in the same futuristic concerns as "stress" – that hadn't been invented either, so we didn't worry about it. Worries were about aplenty, but they were specific, down to earth, real and recognized. They weren't covered by the amorphous, modern day, "there's a lot of it about but we can't always put our finger on it," blanket called stress.

Having a regular supply of coal was a real bonus and a matter of great pride. Coal carried its own images and worth, especially the hard anthracite variety of the west; sombre black in shade but diamond sparkly in colour. My mother always gave me a small lump of anthracite to carry in my pocket for luck, if any test or trial faced me. I had one when I went to sit the 11+ exam in Brynaman Junior School. A successful day would mean grammar school entry. Ah, that lump must have been from a good seam, the black diamond got me through.

So to the black, sombrous, side. I had seen my grandmother cry, really cry, only four times. The first time was when my grandfather was in one of his depressed moods and was off "up the mountain" to do himself mischief. He never did. The second time was shortly after David John, my grandfather's friend and workmate, came to tell her that my grandfather had been killed in the Steer Pit, Gwaun Cae Gurwen, which was an odd quirk of fate bearing in mind his "walks up the mountain".

We, as a family, were there for the third time, when they brought his body home and my grandmother cried, long and very quietly to herself, as the men came into the house. Tears, naturally, came easily on the day of the funeral, but the day that sticks particularly poignantly in my mind was a year later, when I came upon my grandmother in her kitchen, weeping, again –and silently – because she had no coal in the house. In those days, you see, if a miner was killed, the widow would receive one sympathy load of coal, and then the supply stopped.

A CUT ABOVE

'IF IT IS TO be, it is up to me … if it is to be, it is up to me'.

Now there's a mantra that can oil your motivational engine. Just go the extra mile, think of Edison – he may have invented the electric light bulb, but it was the man who invented the meter who made all the money.

I've heard all the motivational jargon but as a boy growing up on the eastern edge of Carmarthenshire, standing astride the line that separated the northern edge of the South Wales coalfield from the brooding bulk of the Black Mountain, the motivational doctrine was quite clear.

'Up to you, mind, but if you don't graft at school, we can order your pit boots now.'

There was always encouragement then, to move on, move out, move up and fly the family flag in professions and pastimes beyond the coalfield, beyond the bath in front of the fire and the "lean to" corrugated scullery, which pretended to be a dining room cum fitted kitchen.

Performance and persistence were the "doing" words to keeping your attainment level high, the standard constant, and being just "a cut above".

Performance came in all guises, from the

classroom weekly or end of term tests, in academic subjects, to the exciting stage shows or concerts.

My first step on the performance stage was at the Aelwyd in Brynaman on St David's Day, when I was in the infant school. We were lined up in costume and each class member had to play his part in an "action song". I was a postman and when my turn came, I duly recited,

'Postman ydwyf I, yn mynd o dy i dy, dyma lythyr mawr i chi, tara ta tym tym ti.'

'I am a postman, going from house to house, here's a big letter for you.'

To be fair, I feel it does lose more than a little in the translation.

In the junior school, when the National Eisteddfod came to Ystradgynlais in the 1950s, I was chosen for the group recitation gang. We practised for weeks. The plan was to recite "Addysg, addysg, rhaid cael addysg", "Education, education, we must have education", while dressed in P.E. kit and building ourselves up into a tableau or pyramid as the poem unfolded.

I had to climb up and balance on Michael Lloyd and Meidrim Barrett, who were down on all fours. At the start of the second verse, a girl named Avril had to throw herself up into a handstand and I had to catch her ankles. She wore, like all of us, floppy shorts, and, in the weeks of training, while looking down in mid-recitation at Avril throwing herself at me, with shorts akimbo, I felt I came to know her very well.

Academic performance was the pinnacle and main thrust however and, the great threat heading towards us in the Primary school was the "Eleven plus" exam. Success led you to the Grammar school; failure pointed you to the Secondary Modern school. There was no continuous assessment it was a "one day winner takes all" trial.

Mam had used all the incentives.

'If you pass, you'll get a bike. Don't forget now, the grammar school uniform is brown. You've always looked good in brown, the secondary modern school's uniform is navy blue, and navy blue has never done anything for you.'

There was another avenue of endeavour, however, a trip to Gwaun Cae Gurwen. If it was felt you had promise but were not firing on all cylinders in school, there was something that could be done. In Gwaun Cae Gurwen there was a woman, a kind of earth mother, who was adept at all the "old ways and remedies".

One of her specialities was "Torri'r Llech", a loose translation meaning to break or repair rickets, a disease affecting the bones in children. It was believed to go much further, of course.

In the context of the "enhanced academic performance" visit, the procedure was simple. You'd be taken to her front room, allegedly, where she had a bowl of hot water, a towel and a sharp knife. She made a small cut in the lobe, or behind the ear, the belief being that, once the blood flowed, all the innate capabilities within you were released. You could become an Einstein overnight, but if you were very "slow", "thick" or "twp", she would cut both sides for you.

I never visited the lady myself but, had I shown any sign of merely cruising in class, the threat was always there. As it happened, I did pass the 11+ for the grammar school, but I often think of what might have been had I been "done" in Gwaun Cae Gurwen. Perhaps I would have been an astrophysicist or brain surgeon by now. A chance missed then, to really be a "cut above".

BE FAIR SIR, BE FAIR

I don't care how old you are, if a teacher was unfair or unkind to you, even in the infant school, you will remember it for ever.

My scar-making incident happened in the junior school. In every end of term test, I had always been beaten by Denzil Jones and Mair Thomas, but in the fourth year I was on the edge of destiny. Going into the last test, General Knowledge, I was lying third again, so I needed two more marks than Denzil and Mair to get level and three more marks than them to get to 'top of the class'. I was strong in General Knowledge, so it was all to play for. The teacher also said, "Now, in this test of twenty questions, spelling will not matter. If the answer is clearly correct, you will get the mark."

The test went well and when the results came back, I had two more marks than Denzil and Mair, so we shared the 'top of the class' spot. Hooray, I was well chuffed ... until I looked at the returned papers. In answer to the question, "What is the highest mountain in Britain?" I put down Ben

Knevis …Nevis … with a silent K, and it had been marked 'incorrect'. I challenged the teacher, who was a long-term temporary staff member from way down the valley. After all, he had said that spelling didn't matter if the answer was patently correct and that answer would have given me the magical three marks to beat my rivals.

"Ah yes," he said, "you're quite right, but you were all so close, I didn't like to separate you." I was dumbstruck. My one chance of being 'top of the class', in all my junior school years, gone … gone in a puff, gone in the whim of a teacher who was, I felt, unfair. That was some years ago, but does the injustice remain? I should say.

A FACILITY FOR A FAUX PAS … HAVE CLANGER, WILL TRAVEL

Llandeilo 1960 and my first close encounter with confusing cuisine – a jacket potato. I was very friendly with a girl from Crescent Road and her parents had, obviously, decided to check me out by inviting me to a dinner party at their house. Such things were alien to my circle of experience. Dinner parties to my knowledge didn't arrive in Brynaman until the late 1970s and prawn cocktail was really a slow starter.

To be fair, her parents had considered my possible discomfort, because Crescent Road, Llandeilo, was dripping with social elite, a few of the residents' off-spring being in private schools. A smattering of those would be at the dinner party, so, to balance things up, it was suggested that I bring a friend. Gareth Jones, a future Director of Education for Ceredigion, was given the job of being my "minder". The fact that he came from Llandeilo Road, in Brynaman, was, I thought, a good omen.

All went reasonably well, until the entrance of something unfamiliar to Gareth and myself. Up until 1960 I had met potatoes in many guises, mashed, chips, new, roast, even potatoes with eyes in them, but never, ever, a jacket potato. And a sliced and decorated one at that. I had been concentrating on the cutlery when it made its entrance. It was my first dabble with a setting of three knives, three forks and two spoons and I messed up at step one, using my desert spoon for the soup. Between courses my eyes were darting lasers, switching from left to right, checking to see what the others were doing, trying not to make my surveying too noticeable.

I was in good company for Gareth was looking intently at the jacket potato as well. We didn't even know it was called that, until one of the others asked, as he passed the plate to me, 'Would you like a jacket potato?'

Gareth was a man of intellect, a miner's son of admirable qualities, an academic, our school rugby XV hooker, and a fine, pure chapel boy. Just prior to that helpful manoeuvre from down the table, of passing the potatoes in jackets, Gareth, in desperation, had drawn deep from his educational pedigree, leaned towards me, and whispered, 'What the hell are those?'

BISHOP'S MOVE TO CHECK

Experience, they say, allows you to recognize a mistake when you make it again. I'm more inclined to the view that experience is frustrating, you get it just after you need it.

I could have done with it in 1974, when I was the Headteacher of Ysgol Thomas Stephens in Pontneddfechan. I had been invited to Ystradfellte Church, to attend the confirmation of a few of the school pupils, in the presence of the Bishop of Swansea and Brecon. The church was packed and Elaine and I sat at the back, in the very last pew. The service went as planned and the Bishop invited everyone to partake of Holy Communion.

There is a difference in procedure between churches and chapels. In church, you have to go up to, and kneel on the rail at the altar. In chapel, the deacons distribute the bread and communion wine to the members in their seats. Elaine and I decided to accept the bishop's kind invitation and, in turn, we joined the queue for the rail. As headteacher of one of the participating schools, I was desperate not to make a mistake, but from my position I couldn't exactly see how it was conducted.

Elaine, eventually, knelt at the rail, but there was no room for me. I was last in the queue, so rather than receive Holy Communion on my own, I knelt next to Elaine and pushed her along the rail a bit and balanced on the end. The Bishop came along the rail, distributing the bread and, as he came to me, my leg slipped off the rail and my hand shot upwards. In confusion, the Bishop thought I was returning the bread and he took it back off me. Elaine, thinking it was a church custom, gave her bread back as well. The Bishop leant towards me and, quietly, whispered,

'You're not from this church are you?'

Fair play to him, he sorted it.

HERE DOGGIE, DOGGIE

Dame Barbara Cartland was a remarkable woman. A BBC Wales television crew had been granted an audience with the grand lady, and I was accorded the privilege of chatting to her.

She was well turned out, even at nine o'clock of a morning, dressed entirely in pink, with a flowing, formal gown and hair and make-up in place. She had a discipline that governed her day and had seen her produce over six hundred novels, at a chapter a day. A novel a fortnight, when in full flow. Many of the front cover designs of her publications had been enlarged, framed and mounted along the corridors and walls of the house. She had two secretaries, one to deal with her administration, in the morning, and the other to take dictation for her stories, a little later.

Dictation lasted two hours, almost exactly so each day, however well it was going. We were allowed to film some of it. 1 p.m. she lounged back on her settee, and started to speak, along the lines of

Madeline stood at the rail of a boat, looking out at the far horizon. The sea was calm, like glass, with the shimmering, setting sun stretching out to paint

the last colours of the day. She felt, deep within her, a longing. Charles had been away too long, she needed him. Her heart ached for his nearness, her body longed for his embrace. She had only met him that spring but she instantly knew. In his Major's uniform, standing next to the great oak tree by the lake, his blue eyes had washed over her in a glance, his hand had held hers, lingering just that extra moment in the touch, when they were introduced. As she let her mind re-live that first, fateful, blushful day, she was aware of closing footsteps behind her on the deck and the familiar scent of male cologne. Her heart skipped a beat, she turned ...

'3 p.m. Finish.'

Extraordinary, Dame Barbara Cartland was able to carry on the following day, apparently holding the scene, mood and fluidity easily in mind.

She invited us to stay for tea.

'You must be famished,' she said. 'Chef will be displeased if you don't eat everything he's prepared for you.'

The dining room table was a delight of sandwiches, cakes, biscuits, tea, coffee and cordials.

As we settled about the table to eat, Dame Barbara started to move the plates around and began regaling us with tales of her life and times. It was all going convivially well, until she became quite animated about the girlfriend of one of the Royal Family.

'I told Her Majesty ... I don't hold with his choice, Ma'am, no good will come of it. Young men must be guided in these matters. I know her family, it's not a good match, believe me.' She took a quick sip of tea, and continued, 'Would they listen? No, and look what's happened now. Too late to close the stable door now, the horse has bolted. I told them. I told them.'

All this was riveting but, in her enthusiasm and passion for the tale, she had stopped moving the plates around and we were still peckish. I saw a plate of biscuits near my right hand and, checking to see that she wasn't looking in my direction, I sneaked one. It was very nice. I went for a second – felt she saw me, so I picked up the plate and, in courtesy, offered her one.

'No, no, no,' she recoiled, 'they're for the dogs.'

I looked down and two terriers were looking up at me. When you're in a hole, you have to stop digging, there was nothing I could say or do. The rest of the BBC Wales gang took note though … I was in several Sunday papers the following week.

PRAISE BE

It's like the start of a joke …

'There was Lord Andrew Lloyd Webber, the Archbishop of Canterbury, Sir Cliff Richard and me, sitting on this settee …'

Fact.

I was chosen as a co-presenter with Pam Rhodes and Don Maclean for the first "Songs of Praise" of the New Millennium, to be held at the Millennium Stadium in Cardiff. It was a privilege and an occasion I shall cherish in the memory for ever. It went superbly well, with Bryn Terfel in a leather trench coat, singing magnificently, Sir Cliff Richard overcoming a dose of influenza to dazzle the congregation, choirs, harpists, Lord Andrew Lloyd Webber gracing the scene, absolutely wondrous.

In fact, Lord Andrew Lloyd Webber had been so taken and impressed with the event, that he set up a surprise dinner party for John Forrest, the Producer of "Songs of Praise" and the presenters were to be included. I still have his invitation at home. What a night!

We gathered at his London home, to be taken up a few floors in a lift and there to meet, amongst others, the Archbishop of Canterbury, Dr. George Carey and his wife, Sir Cliff Richard, Reverend Ernie Ray, Head of Religion at the BBC, Lord Andrew Lloyd Webber and his wife – John Forrest and his wife, to their surprise, joined us later, thinking they were coming to a BBC event.

In all we were about a dozen around the dining room table. I can't remember the menu, but pasta and a tomato sauce appeared at one point. I looked at my white shirt and Elaine's voice rang in my ears,

'Put your napkin in your shirt collar, you know you and sauces.'

In company like that, you can't, can you? You can't put your napkin in your shirt collar. If I'd had a proper, silver, napkin holder, it would have been different.

The conversation was surreal; I couldn't believe that I was in such company. Sir Cliff was easy in conversation, telling me about Radio 2 refusing to play his records.

'Listen now, Cliff,' I said, 'don't you worry about Radio Wales, you'll be played there until the cows come home, every day.'

The Archbishop was tidy, if a little formal, couldn't loosen up with his wife there I suppose.

Actually, I found Lord Andrew Lloyd Webber rather formal and a little bit stiff until I asked him, 'How long have you been married now then?'

He looked across at his wife – a lovely, friendly girl, and asked her for the answer.

'Six months less than you were to Sarah Brightman, so far.'

He laughed, relaxed, so I ventured further,

'There's a nice house you've got here, Lord Webber.'

'Really, do you like it? Come and have a look around.'

He led us up to another floor, pointing out the Canalettos hanging on the walls.

'That's rather a nice one that,' he said. 'I want to make Christmas card copies of it and superimpose the London Eye on the scene, rather fun I think.'

On the top floor, he pressed a button and a section of the roof opened to the sky. He also invited us into a small, private theatre, to view his latest show, in preparation, "The Beautiful Game" about the troubles in Ireland, using soccer as a theme.

It was an extraordinary evening, shame to leave really. Finally, we all collected our coats and headed for the lift. As I swung on my over-coat, I caught sight of it in the mirror, near the door.

There it was, a reddish stain on my shirt, forming a line next to my tie, just where a napkin would have been. Perhaps no one noticed, no one mentioned it anyway, but Elaine would have been mortified. I checked it again. No doubt about it, a Canaletto on the wall; cannelloni on my shirt.

END OF THE ROAD, WELL, STREET ANYWAY

I LIVED FOR ELEVEN years, in Chapel Street, an end of terrace house, which made it semi-detached, so that was a step up. It used to be No 11, but then it changed to 22, without being moved. Times were hard, but I didn't realise that, because it was a happy home and most of my friends were in the same boat. We had no furniture in one downstairs room for five years, our bathroom hung on a nail, on an outside wall, near the back door and our semi-detached toilets were three yards from the backdoor near the single, shared, cold-water tap. My father worked nights regularly, so I slept with my mother until I was 10. When my father returned from night shift, he always had a warm bed to get into at eight in the morning.

We had a long garden that ended in a chicken run, near the lilac tree at the edge of the dividing wall with Gibea Chapel cemetery. On the main road side, the retaining wall of the cemetery was 15 feet high, so most people, years ago, were not buried 6 feet down in Gibea, but 9 feet up.

It was in that house that I first became aware of the different social standing between men and women. Women were always assured of more privacy. When my father had a bath in front of the fire after coming home from the Steer Pit, our neighbour, Mrs Catura Price, would often come in to borrow sugar, butter or whatever. My father didn't seem to mind. He'd go down in the water a little bit, for discretion's sake and Mrs Price would walk straight past him, with just a quick acknowledgement.

However, when Mrs Price had a bath, all doors were locked, curtains were drawn and all children sent to another street to play. Why was that, I wonder?

Weekly, there was a lovely smell from the Price's house when she baked bread, and she had something that I considered a treasure trove, a Grattan Mail Order Catalogue. There were wondrous things in there, especially in September, when all the Christmas gifts and toys were listed and shown in photographs. Later in life, as I've said elsewhere, my initial sex education came from looking at pages 76 to 94 of the Grattan Mail Order Catalogue.

Bath nights were Sundays or, sometimes Fridays. The bath was put on the floor, near the black-leaded grate and coal fire, so that your belly got searing hot and your back, facing the draught from the door, was freezing cold. The semi-detached toilets had only a single brick thickness separating them so, sitting there, you could have a chat with Rhys Price from next door if he was in theirs. Toilet paper was the Daily Herald – cut into squares if you were posh.

I once related that tale at a Historical Society

meeting in Merthyr Tydfil. A local author came up to me afterwards, and stated that their family had the same arrangement in Merthyr, and that she did her occasional courting in the toilet. She was courting the boy next door, and in those days there was nowhere to go on a wet night, so she would arrange to go to her toilet at seven o'clock and he would do the same in his toilet. He, being a boy of some eager ingenuity, had knocked three bricks out of the wall so they could hold hands while they talked.

Now, there's a lateral thinker, I bet he ended up in brain surgery, or advanced physics – or, most probably, architecture.

DROPPING OUT OF SCHOOL IN UPPER BRYNAMAN JUNIOR – LITERALLY

Upper Brynaman Junior School had burned down prior to my time there. Consequently, we were taught in temporary buildings. When I was in Standard Two, Mr Rheinallt Thomas's class, a man suddenly opened the classroom door, looked totally bemused and then apologised.

'Sorry, I thought it was a café.'

Mr George, the headmaster, had his study in the middle of the playground. It was a green shed and, if you went there, you found that inside, there was a smell of ink and old books and, on wet days, drying macs.

Two canes leaned against the wall. It was well known that Mr George took no prisoners, so you really didn't want to go to the green shed, even on an errand. It was the school's "Check-point Charlie" a "no go" area – not without a permit anyway.

Mr Bevan, who taught the third year, was also in charge of music in the school. He had a low threshold of tolerance, his blood pressure was always on "simmer", and when it blasted, the veins at the side of his temples bounced in a kind of rhythmic throb.

Miss Hannah Williams was in charge of the fourth year Scholarship class that prepared you for the 11+ exam and entry to secondary school. She was a good teacher, but I was afraid of her. She was innovative in that she sometimes ran a kind of mentoring system, whereby the able children sat next to those having some trouble with their arithmetic sums. We had loads of homework and I still have the books at home now, with pages of long division and long multiplication sums that seemed to go on for ever. You could only get two sums on a page. Area sums could be longer, because you had to draw the figures as well, in working out the area of a path around a lawn, seeing that you were given the dimensions of the lawn and path and the dimensions of the lawn without the path. They weren't hard, but they took hours to do.

One day some six weeks before the 11+ examination, we all had to line up at Miss Williams's desk. As I got nearer, I kept hearing the question, "And what parish?" I thought she meant which chapel or church do you go to? I was mortified, because we were not a big chapel family, how could I say "No chapel at all, Miss"?

I was only one place in the queue from her, with panic and shame fighting for a place in my mind and knees, when it suddenly became clear that her query was not ecclesiastical but local authority geographical. The relief on my face must have been apparent over three rows of desks. "Which council parish do you live in Roy, Quarter Bach or Llandeilo Fawr?"

I almost shouted out in joy, "Quarter Bach, Miss. Quarter Bach."

Two things still stand out about the 11+ day. In the mental arithmetic test, we had ten minutes to answer ten questions. I flew nine in five minutes, but, for the life of me, I couldn't do the tenth. In the "meanings of words" section of the English paper, there was a question, "What is a florist?"

I didn't have a clue. There was a house with large glass greenhouses on our road, we regularly bought tomatoes and cucumbers there and, as children, we'd often go there for mini-tomatoes which couldn't be sold but, no one had ever called it by a name other than "hot-houses". They did sell flowers but, only as wreaths, bouquets were decades away from being fashionable. In desperation and in answer to the question, "What is a florist?" I put down – someone who cleans floors.

When the results of the 11+ came, the announcement was cruel. Mr Talbot Davies, who was the Headmaster by this time, came into the class, stood at the front, and said that he would read out the list of the successful pupils who had passed for the grammar school. In the class, there were a few who had been expected to pass, so their disappointment must have hit the depths of their very being. Of course, for us, the successful ones, it was euphoria – contained euphoria mind – because the teachers would not have it otherwise. Eight of us made it. Just eight.

After the announcement, the newly announced grammar-school pupils were allowed to go home immediately to tell their parents. I flew along Chapel Street, jumped down from the wall behind the house to find my mother in the coal-shed. Before I could say anything, Mrs Catura Price, from next door, saw me and shouted, 'Sadie, he's passed the 11+, I bet.'

My mother was beaming – black from the coal-shed dust but beaming. My father was on night shift, so she got him out of bed. He gave me half a crown, not bad when you think his weekly wage was only £6.

The excitement had to be contained when realisation of those who had failed came back to mind. In the houses of those who had been expected to pass, but hadn't, there was a deep disappointment and hurt. It was almost a grieving and, if curtains had been drawn, in the same way as happened at a death, I wouldn't have been surprised.

There was so much importance attached to that examination, it was a dominating, almost unreal expectation and weight upon the child. It was also divisive, because, from then on, we'd be going to different schools, brown uniform for the grammar school; navy blue for the others in the secondary school.

When we finally left the junior school, Miss Hannah Williams wrote in our autograph books. They were much in vogue then, but I'd forgotten mine, so she wrote on a piece of paper, "Memories will give you roses in December." I still have the paper now.

SPIDERMAN I AM NOT

I once fell out of school – literally. Well, "fell off" would be a more accurate description. On a cold, starlit, winter's night, when I was thirteen and out with the "gang", boredom set in and someone had the bright idea of playing commandos on the flat roof of the junior school outbuilding. It was quite an adventure, because there were night classes being held in the school, which added to the "dare".

We climbed up a metal ladder attached to the wall and clambered all over the flat roof, ducking and hiding, just in case any enemy would see this early bunch of the SAS. Suddenly, one of the boys shouted, 'Someone's coming.'

We shot back towards the ladder. I was running at an angle without realising it and, just like Tom in a "Tom and Jerry" cartoon, my pounding legs hit thin air … and I dropped into the girls' playground. I still don't remember the incident clearly, nor the pain, for I was knocked out.

The boys, fair play to them, tried to find me in

the darkness but to no avail. They went to Penycae Shop, bought matches and continued the search. I came "round" to their whispered shouts of 'Roy, Roy oh' and, to the, gradually, clearing images of lighted matches and stars in the sky.

When the boys found me, they ran to one of the classes in the night-school – a First Aid class. That class must have thought it was Christmas, a ready-made, to your door, real casualty. I remember their concerned queries, 'Where does it hurt? Can you move your leg? Can you speak?'

All very reassuring except for the local policeman, also a member of the First Aid class, who came out with, 'What were you doing on the roof?'

I ended up in Morriston Hospital that night. The first diagnosis, from a first year intern probably, was fractured skull, two broken arms, broken leg and smashed teeth. The following morning, it was re-adjusted to two broken wrists and smashed front teeth.

WHO'S GOT MY COAT?

I visited the old school recently. The temporary buildings have gone. The playground is a car-park for the new Village Centre, which has been developed from the old infant school across the road from where Brynaman Junior School used to be. The village has a new primary school now. When I was accorded the honour of officially opening the first section of the Centre, the memories came flooding back.

I could still see in my mind, the cloakroom, from which my new, navy blue, gabardine mackintosh had been taken, clearly by mistake at the turmoil of "home time" but it was never returned, much to my mother's pique. I hope it went to a good cause and that it was worn in good health, that's all I can say.

At the side of the road entrance to the Centre, where the school railings had been, was the spot where I'd stood, with lips quivering in self pity, for missing out on pudding in school dinners. When the dinner lady shouted, 'Who hasn't had pudding?', I had been too shy to answer. As luck would have it, my mother was passing the school, saw me, and went to Pen-y-cae shop to get me a small bar of chocolate. I was right for the afternoon then and went back to happily playing chariots with the boys, – a game where two boys pulled a third around the yard, sending sparks flying from their hobnailed boots, the fashion statement footwear of the time.

The new café was Mrs Morgan's old classroom, where we spent so much time getting our daps out of the cupboard for PT lessons – Physical Training. It easily took twenty minutes to find a left and right shoe, of the correct size and with laces in both. The verrucca had not been invented then, so we were all right on that score.

Across the corridor had been Miss Griffiths's class where we painted doilies at Christmas time and made endless trimmings from coloured paper.

In the corner had been the headmistress's room, Miss Llewellyn. Ah, dear Miss Llewellyn. It was in her room that we had the embarrassing medicals and it was there I first came across the yellow school dentist's forms. When the dentist was due at the school, you were given blue or pink forms, for the boys and girls. After the examination, those needing treatment were given a yellow form.

It was always bad news if your name was called and you were given a yellow form. The treatment vied between passable and primitive. I remember treatment in a power cut, when the dentist's drill was not working and he had volunteers to drive it on a pedalling system. On the extraction front, I can still hear the crack of my tooth, as he pulled it out, just as I was coming out of the gas anaesthetic.

'Sorry, lad,' he said.

Sorry! Sorry! I had a blood clot for two days and I was on "Bara Te" a bowl of bread and warm tea, for a week.

One rose-tinted memory takes me back to Miss Llewellyn's room. It was to be my very first day in school. Mam took me down. She had tried to build up the excitement for me, but I was suspicious. I was unconvinced, I was happy enough at home, I was no trouble.

Miss Llewellyn called us in.

'Sorry Mrs Noble,' she said. 'We haven't got room. You'll have to bring him back next term.'

Now, have you ever tried to walk along a road, elated, bursting through your vest at happy news, yet holding back a smile, in case your mother would see – and trying desperately not to skip … it's not easy, but I managed it.

SEX EDUCATION

IN EARLY PUBERTY DAYS, boys, whose sap was showing signs of movement, were beset by an itching curiosity. Unless you had several sisters, the mechanics and geography of the female form was a mystery. There was very little in the way of "visual aids" about. There were no naughty videos but the search for carnal knowledge was helped, significantly, by photographs in the *Health and Efficiency* magazine. They were black and white photographs, but they fitted the bill.

Acquiring the magazine was the thing. A strategy of subterfuge, requiring clandestine planning and execution, was put in place by the committee, or gang and, as an extra phi of excitement and daring, a 'lottery' element was included. Whoever drew the "short straw" had to go into the shop to buy it.

Looking back, the magazine was a tame publication. All the photographs, of unclothed women were set in sand dunes or forests and, very tastefully turned out. To us though, young bucks of the parish, they were rampant raunchiness. They were visions of promise beyond the far horizon.

To safeguard secrecy it was necessary to travel from the village to make the 'hot' purchase; the Brynaman Post Office didn't carry it anyway.

'Hades' was the town of Ammanford and it required a special trip, for, although we all went to Ammanford secondary schools, no one thought it a good idea to buy it in our dinner hour, in uniform, and then file it in someone's satchel. No, a special expedition had to be arranged by train, not a bus; buses were too public. Non-corridor trains of the type plying the G.W.R. Ammanford to Brynaman line, offered safety away from prying eyes.

Michael drew the short straw, but we were all behind him in spirit and body – well, up to the newsagent's door in The Arcade anyway. Michael was a good choice, because he did 'nonchalant' better than the rest of us and, having sprung up early in puberty, height and spots, he could reach the top shelves without giving the impression that he was over-stretching himself.

Hiding it in "Biggles" books or an "Eagle" comic became an art form that MI5 would have rubber-stamped in effective efficiency. Moving it around "the gang" was a slight-of-hand marvel.

Health and Efficiency moved us on. After a year's supply of that magazine, we had the theory cracked.

The practical, however, was still an adventure away.

The only sex education in my day, apart from *Health and Efficiency* was a surreptitious look at pages 76 to 94 of the Grattan mail order catalogue when your mother was out.

Things have changed. Judging by the levels of promiscuity these days, the theory into practice interlude is a mere hop, skip and a jump.

Good grief, where has the mystery gone? What about the thrill of the chase? In my day if a boy went out on a date his mates always quizzed him as to what had happened. How far he got? How many degrees had been registered on the carnal thermometer? He'd always lie – of course.

'I tell you, boyo, if the bus hadn't come early, I'd have been there, all the way.'

Lying was a part of maturing, on the lustful league table anyway.

Oh no, there didn't seem to be too many "the birds and the bees" chats from father to son in my day. Perhaps it was because most houses didn't have parlours, a room where a dad could sit his son down and warn him of the chapel deacon's wrath if he got a girl into trouble.

Fast girls were to be avoided; but I'm sure those poor dabs had a "fast" reputation only because the boys had lied in the first place about how hot a date had been.

I suppose the influence of the chapels, your mother's encyclopaedic and double dire warning: "You be careful, don't you bring trouble back to this house", and the sheer fortress defence of a 1950s roll-on girdle, all combined to dampen the ardour.

I don't envy boys these days. Many of the girls appear to be the predators. Boys are under pressure to perform, allegedly getting "marked out of ten" by the girls for finesse and finality. It must be really intimidating and so difficult to get a pass mark, let alone highly commended.

No, I'm not at all envious. There was a certain

charm in proper courting, whether in the cinema, on a mountainside or in a Ford Anglia.

Elaine and I were allowed to do some courting in her grandmother's front room on Sunday afternoons. It was all done with proper decorum, her grandmother's frequent knocks on the door with yet another cup of tea, saw to that. I think the record was six knocks in two hours. It's no wonder that, after those "tea and courting" Sundays, I moved on to coffee for a few years.

College days offered some freedom from scrutiny, although there was a strict "tutor on duty" surveillance system. That is, until "visiting" was brought in as an experiment. I was the Student Union President in Cardiff Training College at the time and well remember, in 1963, when this new concession of "visiting" was debated at the National Union of Students' Conference in Manchester. Under this adventurous and groundbreaking scheme, boys would be allowed to visit girls' rooms, and vice versa, on two occasions a week. There was to be a two-hour "window of visiting" on Sunday afternoon and an hour and half on a Wednesday evening, both occasions being after heavy meals.

At a later National Conference in Scarborough, the "feedback" report from the platform had a plea from the Trinity College, Carmarthen delegate that visiting should be cut down. It was all too much for them, too distracting, too wearying. Their motion was put to the vote and was not so much defeated as smashed out of sight.

Courting in school days threw up many

obstacles and initiative tests. No one had cars, bus shelters weren't beyond the drawing-board stage and walks on the mountainside offered very little privacy, especially on the wild, open moorland of the Black Mountain in Carmarthenshire, where sheep outnumber trees by about three hundred to one.

If you happened to be going out with a girl who was in the same school as yourself, there were immediate advantages. In the Amman Valley Grammar School there was an accepted strategy, especially on dark, cold winter nights. The girl would make sure, on a Friday afternoon that the latch was slightly off on the girls' cloakroom window. This accommodated entry on the Saturday night if the caretaker or cleaners had not been entirely vigilant.

A Saturday night date would usually begin in "the first house" at the Palace or Welfare cinemas, meeting outside the building, unless the boy was an absolute skinflint and avoided paying for his girlfriend by meeting her inside. Following the film show, phase two of the date was the trek to the school and a quick check to see if the latch on the cloakroom window was still off. If it was, the next step was a swift heave and a climb through the window, ignoring any sounds from within because, a pound to a penny, you were not the first to arrive that night. It was uncertain, in the dark, how many couples there were, but a quick "feed-back" check in school on the following Monday, would give you an educated tally.

Those who were not comfortable with the co-operative, serious, but silent courting scenario in the cloakroom, ventured further into the building and ended up in the Ladies' Staffroom.

I was never that courageous, courting in company was fine by me.

COURTING

THE LANGUAGE OF SWEET NOTHINGS IN MY DAY

IT'S NICE TO SEE the Welsh language flourishing these days. To be honest, my Welsh always was more pavement than eisteddfod platform, more club and institute than chapel pew. It's something I've regretted. Mrs Catura Price from next door did take me to chapel on a few Sundays but Mam never really pushed it. I often wonder why.

I remember debates about language usage during my formative years. One incident took place during a college summer holiday job with Llandeilo Rural District Council. We, my fellow workers and I, were working in a trench outside Llandovery in the Cil y cwm area. We were "the water gang", laying new pipes, and in charge was the foreman, Trevor, from Pennygroes, who was quite a linguist – English, Welsh and two words of Italian. During the war, he had fought with the D-Day Dodgers, as he called them, all the way up the entire leg of Italy, past Monte Casino and Rome, on just those two Italian words, "Quanto costa?" – "How much?"

In that trench was Gareth Jones of Brynaman, later in life to become the Headteacher of Lampeter

Comprehensive school and Director of Education for Ceredigion, John Davies of Llandybie, later to become Honorary Physician to the Welsh Rugby Union with a practice in Harley Street, and me.

One day, the general chit-chat, mattock-swinging and long-armed-shovel-heaving, gave way to a debate on whether, when going out with girls, you did your courting in Welsh or English. Now, after a long discussion and bearing in mind we, all three young bucks of the parish, were going out with Welsh-speaking girls, the vote went to the English language.

Why? Well, in those days, the Fifties and early Sixties, we took our lead from Tyrone Power, Errol Flynn, Jeff Chandler and the like, all seen in films in the Brynaman Public Hall. "I love you" was direct, to the point, no ambiguity. Welsh sentences were longer and we all felt that by the time you got the words out in Welsh, the mood had passed.

Even now, I know of quite a few couples, who are both Welsh-speaking, have children who are Welsh-speaking, they speak Welsh to the children, but cannot speak Welsh to each other, because they did their courting in English.

Tyrone Power and his cronies have a lot to answer for!

SIR WALTER RALEIGH

Take the St David's road from Haverfordwest, and you take in the pleasures of Solva and Newgale Beach. Newgale is a long stretch of sand, banked with pebbles that try to move inland when a heavy storm comes off the sea. It's a breezy, refreshing, cobweb-clearing place.

It's also a place of chivalry and knightly gestures. Well, it was once. On our Amman Valley Grammar School Arts Society (of which I was chairman) trip to St David's, there was a girl who held a certain interest for me, so the "comfort break" at Newgale allowed me a chance to make a tentative move – just to test the water.

As we walked along in a group, we came to several small pools of seawater. One was directly in our path and, it was there that I did my Sir Walter Raleigh bit. Jokingly, yet with as much aplomb as a sixth-former could muster, I put down my coat and said,

'Here we are, don't get your feet wet, just step on my cape.'

She did. The state of the black zipped jacket with tartan lapels took some explaining when I got home.

YOU DANCIN'? YOU ASKIN'?

I thought that dancing was something that only went on in Ammanford. As a little lad, I slept over in my grandmother's house whenever Mam and Dad went off dancing, and when I asked them where they'd been, the answer was always Ammanford.

The word dancing always rekindles a memory of a "sleepover" in Mamgu's, sharing a big feather bed with my uncles Thomas and Illtyd, me being in the middle, in the deep valley of the mattress, upside down to them, with my head between their feet. One particular night is clear in my memory.

Mamgu's lodger, Richard Coleman, known by all as Dick, slept in one of the back bedrooms, he was a south coast of England man, a jobbing brickie and builder, who was a friendly, kindly soul.

On that graphic night, he was very ill and Mamgu and Mam were tending to his needs. I can still see my mother now, wildly coming into our bedroom and saying, 'Dick is dead. He suddenly sat up in bed, demanded a brandy, I gave it to him; he swigged it down in one gulp and collapsed back on the pillow – dead. I think I killed him!'

In my mind, dancing and death are strange bedfellows, but they're there. If the memory files things under subject headings, it must have a strange indexing system.

My own initial dancing experience centred on the St David's Day eisteddfod in Amman Valley Grammar School. I was in the Llewellyn House country dancing team. I still have the chapped thigh marks from the lederhosen.

We were told that, on stage, whenever we were near Miss Norman, Head of PE for girls and the country dancing competition judge, we were to smile. Whatever our discomfort, a smile was worth extra marks, so 'Think happy thoughts' was the directive from our dance tutor.

Miss Norman was to feature large in the later years of grammar school. In the Sixth Form, in preparation for the Christmas party we were frogmarched to the gymnasium, twice a week, from September to December for compulsory ballroom dancing lessons. Nobody was let off, unless they had a broken leg and, even then, they had to bring a "to be excused" note from their mother.

It was a lottery, in that boys were lined up against one set of gymnasium wall-bars and the girls were lined up on the opposite side. One boy had the foresight to count along his line and then to count the girls to find his partner. A –

'God, look who I've got!'

Said it all, about his disappointment. He turned in desperation to the boy at his side, 'Colin, be a sport, change places with me, I'll give you half a crown.'

The great bonus in those lessons was that the dance teachers were the PE Heads of Departments. Mr Adams, Head of PE for boys, was a marvellous man, in the autumn of his teaching career; he was in his early fifties. Miss Norman, on the other hand, in charge of the girls, was in the early spring of hers; she was in her early twenties.

The great joy for a boy of 16, 17, or 18 years of age was that, if you couldn't do a waltz, tango, Gay Gordon's, or quickstep, Miss Norman would come and help you and, hold you close. Now, when the good Lord gave out female attributes, she must have been in the front of the queue for everything. One dip and turn in a tango with Miss Norman would advance a young boy's education by several years.

After we married, Elaine and I did attend dance lessons, but the very good tutors from Ystrad Mynach went and left us, in mid cha cha cha, for a contract on a P&O liner cruise to South Africa.

73

I also found one aspect of their tuition confusing. They would line up all the men at one end of the dance-floor, all the ladies at the opposite end and, to the musical direction of "One, two, three, one two three ...", each group approached the other in a big bunch. It always ended up in a melee in the middle.

Dancing remained a resolution. I decided, some years ago, to concentrate on just one New Year's resolution each year. One was to gain my bus driving licence, which was duly completed. Another was to learn the Argentinean Tango, a dance I've always coveted. My tuition was filmed for S4C.

I confess the Argentinean Tango was too much for me. My partner, a magnificent dancer from Llanelli, was too lithe and powerful. When she wrapped her leg around my thigh, all the blood was cut off to my ankles, causing numbing pins and needles. I had to withdraw to the waltz and jive. Actually, I thought I was always pretty good at the jive, but Elaine tells me that the doyen of jiving is Dai Latham, who keeps the Gloucester Arms in Aberdare.

Once a year we attend a cancer charity Christmas event at the Masonic Hall in the town, not that I'm a Mason, but it's a welcoming venue. Dai, the jive doyen, is always there with his wife, but Elaine makes sure that she has a few dances with him. He is good, to be fair. It wouldn't be so bad, but Dai is famous for having bad feet. He always struts his stuff wearing daps, even if he's wearing a posh suit.

A FAIR TO REMEMBER

HIS NOSE WAS BIG – that was the problem! Wherever he went, his nose got there a fraction before him and in the ring of that boxing booth it was a tempting and frequent target for his opponent. The sign outside was clear enough,

LAST THREE ROUNDS OF TWO MINUTES EACH AGAINST OUR NATIONAL CHAMPION, AND WIN £10.

Once "the drink is in, the sense is out", in the same way that when your logic goes to your loins, you're lost. Bravery gets to the brain when the fourth pint makes you Tarzan. Our local hero and challenger was flattened in the second round, his nose hitting the canvas first.

As a boy that was my first visit to a proper booth at Brynaman Fair.

Twice a year, spring and autumn, the Fair came to the village and filled the patch of ground between Siloam Chapel and Ebeneser Chapel with noise, colour and exciting temptations.

There weren't many "rides" but, there were just enough to use up the limited money around. As you got older you graduated from the two small children's roundabouts, with their double-decker buses, fire engines, steam locomotives and cars, up to the Noah's Ark Carousel, where the animals went up and down as they went around. Come to think it – I don't know why we called it "Noah's Ark" because it only had horses on it! "The Stable" or The Cavalry" would have been better names.

The sail boats, or "swings" as we called them, were always down the bottom end of the field, where Gareth kept his buses and coaches. The swings were a favourite of mine, especially if the girls were watching you, because it was showing off time then, sending the swings high, towards the coal tips that rose behind the public toilets. Even the newly invented "pac-a-mac", which was easily wind affected, was no restriction at all.

The "Dodgems" were always called the "Bumpers" in Brynaman and they were the last stop on the maturing trail for youngsters as they became older and braver. It was all very physical and it was always a dash to get a vacant car when they stopped.

Brynaman Fair offered me the first taste of toffee apples, candyfloss and butter-kissed pop-corn. There was a fish and chip stall ,but there was no excitement going there: we had a couple of those in the village all year round.

I was never lucky at the competition stalls, "Roll a penny – Roll a ball – Poke a ticket out of a straw" – but, if you had three consecutive goes without success, the attendant, who was the first man I'd ever seen wearing an earring, gave you a prize anyway.

There was an early bingo or tombola stall but I didn't understand how it worked, so I kept away from it. I wonder if anyone did actually win one of those big baskets at the top of the stall, the ones with the full tea-set inside.

As for the booths, well, you take in the boxing, the Mystic Meg Crystal Ball gazer, unusual exotic animals and, finally, the quiet stalls, those selling rugs, mats and linen.

There was the one booth, though, that stays in the mind, the best ever at Brynaman Fair. It was the "Historical Tableau Exhibition". I couldn't understand why one of our neighbours said to me, 'Hey, you shouldn't be going in there, you're too young.'

But it all became wonderfully clear as we entered the tent. The woman in the tableau was nude. Naked as the day she was born. She posed behind a thin gauze curtain, in various historical character-guises, statuesque, not allowed to move apparently, lest it become deacon-testing sensual. When the thick curtains first opened, she was "Cleopatra at the side of the Nile", holding a basket of fruit. Next came "Boadicea in her chariot", her helmet being her only attire. Then, 'Queen of the Incas' in head bandana and nothing else, and on to 'Josephine – waiting for Napoleon', lounging on a French flag counterpane.

I think it was on that night that my abiding interest in history began; Brynaman Fair was the academy that set me off.

BRYNAMAN CARNIVAL … NOT RIO, BUT A CLOSE RIVAL

A day to step outside yourself … you could be

anything, or anyone, you liked. Cowards could become heroes, a pauper could be king and the timid could become the Pied Piper.

Brynaman took its carnivals very seriously. There was a carnival season, every road had its own cavalcade and, on the fourth Saturday, all roads joined together for the big one. Jazz bands led the parade, with kazoos and kettle-drums filling the air, which was hard work when you were climbing the hill of Station Road. However puffed you were, you had to make an effort when you got to the Post Office. The road turned there and the place was wide enough for a big crowd, so that was the place to really do your thing.

My mother was well into carnival, being a member of the ladies' jazz band under the leadership of Megan Thomas, nee Price, whose mother had lived next door to us in Chapel Street. My uncles, Illtyd and Thomas, were in the Rhos Garw jazz band. A very military band, dressed in smart hussar-style uniform. They practiced their display routine twice a week up on the tips and did the rounds of many carnivals, winning prizes along the way. My favourite jazz band was from the Club and Institute. All the men were dressed in a variety of outlandish comedy costumes, like nightgowns, slinky dresses, Vikings, Desert Rats army uniforms, their leader throwing his long baton into the air and attired in a beret, waistcoat, no shirt, skimpy bathing suit, Wellington boots, with a smoked kipper hanging between his legs.

As for me, well, let me tell you, my mother was an inspiration of design and invention. Mam turned me out as an Arab sheik once, having talked Dai Parry into lending us his horse and Dad into dressing up as half-clown, half-ringmaster, to lead the horse in the parade. I looked the part and, fair play, I won first prize.

The next carnival saw me as an Indian Prince, in silks and gravy browning, walking on my own between two of the lorry carnival floats. I must have impressed, even though my gravy browning was running, for I won first prize again. Mam got a bit cocky after that and entered me in carnivals in other villages, with less success, but that was down to local bias, according to her.

Actually, she kept the Indian Prince outfit for years and Richard, our son, was bedecked in it at one Fancy Dress event – with a lot of protest I have to say – but he won first prize, so Mam was doubly chuffed. Ah, talent and quality will stand the test of time.

THROUGH THE WINDOW TO 'NARNIA' IN AMMAN VALLEY GRAMMAR SCHOOL

I was mortified, after just one week in Amman Valley Grammar School, being given 50 lines for forgetting my Latin text book. Upset? Don't talk! I never recovered. Latin and I parted company at the end of the first year. My "Amo, amas, amat" had really gone all flat.

What intimidated me more than anything was the fact that there appeared to be so many good pupils from Ammanford. I couldn't understand it, were they on better food or what? More vitamins perhaps? Or was it because they didn't have as far to travel to school as us, the bussed "up valley" kids, and could have an extra half an hour in bed? Thank heavens for Derec Llwyd Morgan, who was an 'up valley' Cefn Bryn 'brain' boy, he kept our end up. He was in 2A with me. Amman Valley Grammar didn't bother with classes 1A, 1B or 1C – it was straight to the 2s, so you were given a fair idea of the pressure and expectation.

You could tell straight away that Derec was talented, able and academic. I'm sure he wore thick vests, just to keep his potential warmed up at all times. He was a high flier at 12, absolutely astral at 16 and totally cosmic in the Sixth Form. He ended up as a "Godfather" in Welsh universities. His only flaw, as far as his class-mates were concerned, was that he said he'd had a "calling" as a chapel minister, when he was about 16. No one could find out how the "calling" came. Whether it was a sudden dramatic flash, or crept up on him quietly, but, a year later, he had a greater calling, under a pac-a-mac with a talented, attractive, harpist, on a rainy day at Carreg Cennen Castle. After that, academia was a magnet far more powerful than religion for him and the pulpit played second fiddle to the lecture-theatre lectern. Good man.

I was nearly in the prestigious Sixth Form Christmas play, but, in that same roof fall earlier in my school tenure, I'd knocked out my front teeth. I was a long time getting falsies, so my "gap year" became four years, and I had difficulty saying my esses clearly. Sadly, I was demoted from my part but, because I was doing Art in the sixth form, I was given responsibility for the scenery. I must say, my distribution of the flakes in the snow scene at the window is still talked about today.

It was Narnia in the school hall; such was the drama and effect. It was a long time before "acting" finally got on my CV. Shame really: deep down I do feel there is an untapped reservoir of the "Al Pacino" about me.

PERSONALITY CHANGING WATER IN BRYNAMAN BATHS

Brynaman Baths, or swimming pool, lies alongside the pitch of the Brynaman Rugby Football Club. My first visit was when I was in the primary school. We were taken down as a class to be taught how to swim. The pool was not heated and the first encounter with the water almost parted body from soul, especially at that "aagh" breath-catching, just above the swimming trunks belly line, moment. Goose-pimples burst into view and your eyes roll towards heaven, your entire personality grabbing at any new, more equable, warmer universe.

We had to stand three or four yards from the rail at the side of the pool and then try to make three or four strokes to reach it, before sinking. Several of us didn't quite make it. As I sank, I remember the world turning green. Luckily the water at that end was only about three feet deep. I do feel, however, that the Brynaman Baths water was instrumental in stopping me from being any kind of choir member. It was so cold on the occasions we were there that it had a delaying effect on a boy's maturing processes. Puberty was disorientated by the deadening experience.

By the time it came for pupils to be chosen for the inter-school choir to sing at the National Eisteddfod in Ystradgynlais in the early 1950s, my voice didn't qualify. No teacher could pitch it because it was on a scale beyond the norm. More quadruple cleff than treble. I was sent to the Group Recitation party instead.

A WINDOW ON THE WORLD AT BRYNAMAN HALL

Brynaman Public Hall was my passport to the rest of the planet. There, the world came to our village, twice a week if you could afford it. The first film I can remember was *The Mudlark*, about the little boy who spent all his time on the edge of the Thames and ended up in Queen Victoria's company. When a school group was taken to see *Treasure Island*, Berian Evans hid under the seat when the nasty seaman, Israel Hands, chased Jim Hawkins up the rigging. Mr Jenkins, the cinema manager, always wore a suit and had Brylcreemed hair. He was strict, and kept us all in order. A shout of 'Quiet' shut us all up. Children were allocated the first three rows, unless you were with your mother, then you had free range.

The "features" changed on Thursdays, but the pattern was constant, "Supporting film", the news, either Pathe or Movietone, followed by trailers, adverts – many hand-written if they were local, ice-cream delivery and, finally, the big film. If it was a cavalry versus Red Indians film, we'd very often gallop out at the end of the show, firing our imaginary guns while trying not to fall off our non-existent steeds. Michael Lloyd had a very nasty accident, when his "horse" failed to corner at the Urdd Hall, next to the cinema. Down he went, scratching his knees and mucking up his coat. I knew his mother very well. They lived in our street, so I guessed what he'd have as a welcome at home for dirtying his coat – hot arse and cold tongue.

The Public Hall is in fine fettle still, with a wide stage and screen, which accommodated "Cinemascope" and "Stereophonic Sound" when they first came in. My father, to my knowledge, only went to the cinema once, possibly because he was on constant night shift. He went to see a film about the US Cavalry; I think it was called *The Command*. He became disturbed at the size of the screen and the sounds of the arrows and bullets coming, via stereophonic sound from all over the place, including from behind him. He never went again.

It was also a culture-led entertainment centre. The inter-chapel eisteddfod was held there once a year, over three days, but I was not a great chapel-goer myself and was disappointed not to be involved in it. I wasn't too keen to go as a spectator, because there was always someone who'd ask, 'Which chapel are you from then?'

I was put on the spot once, but Ashley Thomas, a good friend – ended up as a consultant anaesthetist in Haverfordwest – covered for me by saying, 'He goes to church, not chapel, like me.'

Those acts of kindness stay in your mind.

The local operatic society production was always an exciting time. I walked around with an autograph book getting autographs from one or two "stars", who were ordinary people in the village but, once a year, were transformed into princes in Vienna, French Legionnaires in the Sahara or students in Heidelberg.

There was once great controversy amongst the other operatic societies of the valley, because Brynaman had, seemingly, turned semi-professional, in that they had chosen a leading lady from as far afield as Clydach – 12 miles away. There was great rivalry between the operatic societies and they would come and see each other's productions each year, making comments like, 'Yes, very good, but it wasn't as good as our *Student Prince* production of '52'

Bringing in performers from several miles away was really not playing the game and Brynaman ran into trouble again for bringing in a Director from Swansea who, like Alfred Hitchcock, would include himself in a cameo role. He was very good, as I recall, and it was said that his sophistication and natural suavity simply oozed into the orchestra pit when he came on as the boat captain and said, simply, 'Your ship awaits, my lady.'

In the balcony women swooned.

The Brynaman Public Hall is still going strong, and, relatively recently, it received a grant to put new seating in, including, heaven be praised, "doublers" for courting at the back of the balcony.

SPORTING ICON? – IN MY DREAMS

I THINK IT WAS the wartime powdered egg that did
it. It's all very well saying, "You must be positive,
you must look at the land of milk and honey
without distractions of calories and cholesterol,"
but I think that egg clogged my pores.

"Moderation in all things, and manners, too,"
that was a piece of advice that undermined a
competitive edge as well. "Allow others to go first
and life will bring its own rewards." Well, this may
be so, but the top of my sideboard is still empty,
sporting rewards conspicuous by their absence. No
trophies at all, except for the Car Rally Navigator
medal I won for an all night rush in a Mini Cooper
through the Vale of Glamorgan.

The driver was a friend of mine, Denzil Jones,
who was a dentist in the days when pulling teeth
had the ringing bell sound of a money till. It was a
lucrative profession in the Sixties, so he could
afford a Mini Cooper. That car rally was a hard
night. I'm never car-sick but, in a Mini Cooper,
flying around bends, leaping over sudden rises in
the road and with a jolting, lit-up map board
sending your eyes into spasms and your stomach
into convulsions, it's hard to keep a 6 p.m. dish of
faggots, peas and mashed potatoes – with onion
gravy, in place.

I couldn't and didn't. I left bits of Noble, hidden by the night, in picturesque places like Cowbridge, Colwinston, Brynsadler, Llandow, Welsh St Donats – and several other places whose "Welcome to ..." road-signs I couldn't read with eyes that were glazed with a misty longing for a stable settee or a solid, static bed mattress.

Was I ever downhearted? Never. Why? Because I felt needed. I was the great yardstick. All sporting authorities valued me, as a standard gauge, just to show how good the others were. Every parade needs people on the sidelines cheering it on.

However, there were other elements, other ingredients in the formula for my low level of success. Bad luck was one, bad judgement was another and the fact that we didn't have a sporting "selector" of any kind living in our area was a killer blow. Yet, against all adversity, I was a sporting all-rounder. I was mediocre at everything.

Take athletics, in the infant school I was always the runner with the frayed tight coloured chest band, in the lane with a nasty deep trough halfway along its length, leaving me in the dusty wake of the others by the time I came up the slope and out of it.

You couldn't fault my dedication to informal training and fitness, I always loved running. Until that is, the trauma of May 1952 in Chapel Street when I fell while running to Iris's shop and cut a wart off my finger. There was blood everywhere and the "old wives tale" flashed into my mind. "Cut a wart and if blood doth flow, then on those spots more warts will grow."

So it came to pass. For new warts grew where the blood had spilled on my hand. I spent my early puberty years with spots on my face and hard warts on my right hand, warts enhanced as craggy dark mounds because the caustic powder I treated them with turned them brown. I tried everything to get rid of them, even daily doses of spit – to no avail. The age of sixteen proved a catalyst for me, and a telling leap in maturity, for I had my first girlfriend – and my warts fell off.

There was an athletic golden moment too, in the summer of '61. That School Sports Day had started badly. I'd been spiked by Michael Paul Jones as we walked to the 100 yards start. His father was something big in youth clubs and could get proper sports equipment. Michael really looked the part. For a couple of years he seemed to have the only pair of spikes in the valley. He also had a track suit, which was very intimidating. You couldn't compete with that kind of early professionalism, bearing in mind the rest of us had Army and Navy Stores khaki jackets with a towel "round our necks" for effect. When I found out that Michael Paul had actually been training in preparation for Sports Day, that finished me psychologically; I was lucky to come last.

In the mile we were up against one of those irritating boys, William, who must have been in the front of the queue for everything when the good Lord gave out talent. You know the type: four grade A's at A-Level, scholarship winner, Welsh schoolboy rugby cap – and favourite for the mile.

In the race, I spent a depressing six or seven minutes watching his big backside trundle further and further away in a mirage of an Ammanford July afternoon. For four laps he headed south for the horizon, then "round the top of the track" near the old blacksmith's shop, then east for Pantyffynnon. On the last circuit a sudden, chesty surge took him towards Betws Mountain and the tape for an easy victory. My small success was that I'd avoided, by ten yards, being lapped by him

In mid afternoon, the kindly gods took a hand and joy came to pass. In the four by 100 yards relay event I was in the Llewellyn team and yellow was our colour. Both the letter "L" and the colour were very appropriate when worn on my back; "L" for lethargic and yellow indicating my prospective prospects and non-combatant nature. I was anchorman that day, viewing from a distance the flailing progress of the other three team members. Oh, how the sun shone down upon us.

Five seconds after the sound of the starting pistol and only twenty yards into the race, one of the Dewi team fell over; the Hywel team then dropped their baton at the first change-over and one of the Glyndwr team was sick in transit on the third leg. Lo and behold, Llewellyn was in the lead.

I can see him now, Colin Thomas, PhD six years later, coming round the last bend like a frantic, demented "Leaning Tower of Pisa", his eyes wild with effort and clouds of dust coming up from his newly blancoed daps. He looked like a motorised chariot of fire. With a gasping grunt, he stuffed the baton under my arm and I was away.

It was a difficult last leg for me, trying to run the entire 100 yards with my mouth shut to hide the wide gap where my front teeth had once confronted the world. Not easy, especially when you have hay fever as well; you're dying to sneeze and your eyes are watering but, fair play, my nostrils held out and, to the ever-nearing, pounding sound of Viv Williams, of the Glyndwr team, closing the gap, I just managed to get to the tape first. That was the only year that the Llewellyn House won the School Sports. It's a pity they weren't giving out cups.

Swimming, cricket and basketball I can discuss only briefly. In swimming, the early adventures were always in mountain streams or organised junior school class visits to Brynaman open-air swimming pool. The pool was not heated and, as I've mentioned elsewhere, in early May the water temperature could lead to the onset of high-voiced puberty, a good twelve months before the body was ready for it. Still, we persevered, but just as I was mastering the "two strokes and a bubble" technique, they closed the pool indefinitely. They said it was leaking but I think the local council had run out of money.

In cricket, I was lucky to get into the Brynaman Junior School team. Mr Talbot Davies, the headteacher, chose ten boys and I won the toss against Derek Francis for the eleventh spot. We played Garnant Junior School and were hammered 72-22. I scored 2 and dropped a catch.

At Cardiff Training College, I was commandeered to play cricket against Redlands

College, Bristol in 1964 only because the team was very short of players due to the unexpected "shot-gun" wedding of one of the regulars.

I remember Redlands College had a tall, very mature student in his late thirties or well maintained early forties as fast bowler. He looked like an ex-commando who had decided to flirt with teaching as a career after a stint of creeping up on people in the dark in combat areas worldwide. In my cricket performance as tenth man against Redlands, I broke my Garnant Junior School record. I got a "duck" and, maintaining consistency in fielding, dropped a catch.

Basketball record – one game, 1967, in Penarth Grammar School, as a temporary replacement teacher in an exhibition, staff verses students match. The result was an elbow in the nose, a bleeding nostril, not quite a black eye, just a blue and yellow one, and a quick newsreel flash of my early life passing in front of the other good eye. I won't mention the staff versus mixed sixth form netball match of the following term, because I only took the oranges on at half-time.

FIELD OF DREAMS

The great Welsh religious sect: rugby football. Like thousands of other 'would be gladiators of the oval ball' I was very keen, but not much good. It was rugby, or rugby, as a choice in the village or secondary school. In Amman Valley Grammar School, like all similar schools, if any master found out you had been seen playing soccer, you were asked to stand in front of the School Assembly in the morning as an exorcism for your polluted soul.

Soccer was only one step up from hell's ultimate temptation – snooker or billiards. The billiard hall in Brynaman was well scrutineered by "fifth columnists" and spies. You were either reported to the teachers or the chapel deacons, which rendered you educationally beyond the pale and, spiritually, at Hades front doorstep. Like it or not, you were enmeshed in the game and became "confirmed" into that religion.

Even these days, when your body has long since rebelled and demoted you to a passive, yet avid and excitable supporter, if the Welsh international rugby team is doing well, you immediately bond with your gladiatorial side. An inner voice convinces you that, but for a quirk of nature, cursed bad luck, and having no official Welsh selector living in your home area, you would have made it to the top. An automatic choice as a rugby poet on the pitch, surging the pulses at Cardiff Arms Park, or the Millennium Stadium as it is today.

My early student days were spent at Cardiff Training College, which was a kind of Spartan Warrior PE establishment for young men – although the college had been mixed for one year when I arrived. The place had a permanent, heavy aroma of "winter green" or horse-liniment with the outdoor accepted garb being a green tracksuit sporting a silver archer on the heart area of the chest. The place was dripping with poets on the rugby pitch and Lyn 'the leap' Davies, who won an

Olympic long-jumping gold at Tokyo in 1964 and was more than handy in rugby and soccer, was in our year. So, competitive intimidation and a sense of limited sporting possibilities were heavily in the air.

I was not a PE student. Geography was my subject and my only real leaning towards exercise was "field and countryside orientation" – map reading.

The Deputy Principal, Mr Eric Thomas, a wonderful man of standing and standards, had but two gaps in his clear understanding of the human race – the newly accepted female students, and non-PE types. In fact, in the first week of college life, he took all sixteen of us "non green tracksuit wearers" into a lecture room and implored us to conform as well as we could, to endeavour to dress smartly at all times and not make the place unkempt in any way. I prided myself that my chunky fawn cardigan, with the roll-neck collar and large leather buttons, was accepted by Mr Thomas, after an initial two weeks period of frowning-temple uncertainty.

Thomas Gilmour Nimrod Jones, affectionately known as "Spots", from Saron had more trouble passing the "Thomas test" with his rather racy sports-jacket. Spots was his own man and made his mark on the hard, masculine competition front by winning his college colours in fast pint drinking. He was our champion and, his record was 3.5 seconds against the St Luke's College, Exeter, champion.

He still lost, to an incredible "no gullet"

medical phenomena from the south-west. I have another indelible memory of Spots having imbibed far too much on a rugby trip to Brynmawr, feeling wretched on the way home and being held at the open door of the bus as we trundled through Blaina. That was my first experience of seeing 40 mph sick. I hope there wasn't anyone standing at that bus-stop we passed.

I had no chance of being chosen for the college rugby sides, the PE students being such warriors at the game, unless there was gastro-enteritis on the campus. I remember only two such medically affected fixtures, when I played for the Thirds against Abercynon Seconds and against Llandaff North Seconds in the fortnight that the pestilence lasted.

In earlier days, I did manage to pull on the green jersey of my village club, Brynaman, a few times, but again that was usually in the plague months of January and February, when the team was desperately short. On those wintry Saturdays, the village was a dangerous place to be if the team bus was roaming about looking for players. You could have been innocently nipping to the Post Office on a message for your mother, when the team bus, a 29-seater Bedford, came quietly crawling up behind you.

One moment you would be walking the pavement, the next gone – kidnapped to play in borrowed boots, against Llandybie, Briton Ferry, Pontyberem, or even Aberystwyth, with the pork chops for dinner going cold on your mother's table. Many was the time when I was playing on one wing and Gareth, the bus driver, on the other. There were pockets of talent in the Brynaman team, particularly the Seconds team, where I spent most of my time. Berian Evans filled one such talented pocket, when he played as a centre three-quarter. Mediocre as a centre, but what a violinist.

The one good try I scored in Wales, the other was in England, when I was doing missionary work as a teacher '64 to '66, featured Berian Evans. It was against Bishop Gore Grammar School Seconds. Berian, with a typically brilliant display of lack of concentration, found himself, like a roving spy, in the middle of the opposition's back division when they started a passing movement.

By mistake, they passed the ball to him, he turned round, shot the other way, and passed it to Derec Llwyd Morgan (PhD), who grew to be a godfather in Welsh universities and the National Eisteddfod of Wales. Derec, who had a way with words, drew on his deep literary acumen, and shouted, 'Roy, Hoi!'

Lo, it came to pass, or at least he did, and I scored under the post when no one was looking. I should have kept a few blades of good grass from that field, just for memory's sake.

I still think about that try.

A golden moment in the green shirt of the Brynaman First Team, when they were again very short of players, was against Bynea. Three Welsh selectors were present. Why? Well, Terry Davies, the iconic and legendary Welsh full-back, had recently retired from 'first-class' rugby football and had left the Welsh team selectors entirely in the 'proverbial', there being no natural successor. Terry was still keeping his hand, and kicking boots, in, by playing for Bynea. The selectors came to see him, with the view of selecting him for Wales, straight from the village side. The opposition for the day was Brynaman – with Noble out on the wing

There was a large crowd of spectators and when Terry Davies ran on to the pitch, I took in his considerable ambience with a single glance, but at a secure distance of some sixty yards. He was a colossus, built like an inverted triangle, Californian Redwoods for thighs, hint of natural tan on the cheeks, blonde hair as a beacon in a heavy mist and blue eyes that that would snap knicker elastic at 25 yards.

Our tactics for the game were straightforward. Our committee-man, Dai "Pence" – I never knew how he got that nickname – was to stand at various points of the touchline, with defensive shouts of 'kick it', or attacking cries of 'give it to Raymond'.

Terry Davies did not have an outstanding game, solid yet not spectacular, but the opposing Bynea winger to me did; sauntering past me for a try when I was watching Terry. I have met Terry quite a few times over the years, once quietly having a cup of tea in Cardiff Market on rugby international day. Let me say honestly, he is a man of presence, integrity and inner vision who, as a successful businessman, has done so much for his home village. He knows his patch, and tends it regularly.

WHISTLEBLOWER

Where could I go when my combat days were getting numbered? I was too young to be on the Club committee, so there was only one route that offered "travel expenses, the rugby ethos and, a measure of real control" – refereeing. Of course you have to start at the bottom strata, not so much at the grass roots as at the perma-frost. My one weak foible was over-sensitivity, constantly waking up at night, worrying about "dodgy" decisions, possible uncertain grasp of rugby law on my part and my growing, extensive knowledge of colourful English language adjectives that greeted some of my on-field decisions.

Some games stay in the mind for reasons other than the technicalities and laws of the game. New Tredegar Youth were playing Slough Colts on the morning of an international match between Wales and England. The rain, though heavy, was heading horizontally south towards Bargoed. Just five minutes into the second half, there was a shout from the touchline

'Hoi, ref, ow, ref, ow.'

I turned to the voice.

'The women say that the chicken and chips have come early, can you come off now?'

I consulted with the captains, we viewed the rain, we considered the score, with Tredegar leading by over twenty points – and off we trooped, unanimous decision.

I also think I showed tremendous courage when I accepted a lift in their bus down to the international match in Cardiff that afternoon. As I sat in the front of the coach, a bottle was passed to me from the back. "Fancy a drink ref?" Now I had no idea what was in that bottle … I took a risk … I took a swig. It was bitter ale … thank God.

The referees' monthly meetings were revealing. Under the "points of law" section one week, a referee reported that in his game, on the previous Saturday, he had been knocked over by a runaway horse. He got himself up and promptly penalised the home side for failing to secure the pitch. There was nothing in the Welsh Rugby Union Referees' Handbook to cover such an incident but we all backed his initiative, quick interpretation and resolute action.

I was always intrigued by the reports of senior referees, especially the ones who had dropped almighty clangers in top fixtures and international matches. It didn't seem to bother them at all. Compared to the thickness of their skins, the rhinoceros epidermis is mere sugar paper.

Had I stuck my ground, would I have ever made it to the top flight as a senior referee, officiating in stadia worldwide? Possibly, but my over-sensitivity would have landed me on many a window ledge, in depression, I'm sure. Add to my frailty, my bad back … I have a big yellow streak down it and, oh yes, my varicose vein, that popped up at half-time on the Mountain Ash pitch in 1976 and, things did not augur well.

The mystery of refereeing? Well, that's how to find a committee man when the home team have lost and you are looking for expenses. There were many such days.

All this time, the potential has been lying dormant, innate, but too late. The ration days powdered egg must have had a profound side-effect upon me. Still, the little men of limited sporting skill have their place, as performance markers, so that you can gauge how good the others are. That's been my role all right and, like thousands of other Welshmen, I was very keen, but not much good. If only, if only ... field of dreams ... dream on.

SO YOUNG AND CONFIDENT, WE COULD WALK ON WATER

CARDIFF TRAINING COLLEGE WAS split between two sites, Heath Park and Cyncoed, during my time there. Roath Park Lake was on the direct line between them. The Lake area was a wonderful place for walks and general relaxation and, if you felt more physical, even the odd stint on the rowing boats could hone a young man's mind. I particularly liked spring, when the cherry trees were in blossom.

The winter of 1962/63 was hard and cold, and for many months the lake remained frozen solid. We were able to walk over it and play rugby on it.

I was a student teacher at Cardiff Training College from 1961–1964. It's now part of the University of Wales Institute, of which I'm a proud Fellow. Originally based in the buildings of an old Army camp in Heath Park, the new college buildings were opened at Cyncoed during my time there, and I made many lifelong friends on the two sites. Life was strict, especially at the Heath, where Religious Assemblies were held each morning and resident tutors kept checking on you.

The college concentrated on physical education and most of the students there, on the male side, looked like young gladiators in their green tracksuit, with a permanent odour of liniment about them. Of the 60 or so men in my year, well over 40 were in PE and the rest of us were in the general department, lesser beings as we were. Mr Eric Thomas, Deputy Principal, as I mentioned elsewhere, really did have problems with the two renegade student animals who lived their lives outside the male Spartan sporting discipline ... girls and us ... the slouching non-PE types.

Even our plea that we were, thinkers rather than "doers" fell on deaf ears. So intimidated was I, that after six weeks I felt I had to change my subjects, which were originally Geography and Art. In the art class there were 15 women and myself. I stuck it out until we got to embroidery, then I was gone in a cloud of dust. I changed to History and also started studying the Rugby Football Union laws, so I could qualify as a referee and get some kind of credibility in that Spartan warrior factory.

I did manage to play for the college at rugby football, but only when many of the young gladiators were unavailable for selection. To be fair to my student friends on the PE wing, at the end of the first year, they elected me as their student representative and, at the end of the second year I became the Student Union President.

In that capacity I was able to visit many conferences throughout the land and, for the first time, was able to speak publicly from various platforms. It was my first crack at trade unionism, and I enjoyed it.

UNDER THE BOARDWALK IN ABERYSTWYTH

I have to include Aberystwyth on my itinerary of memory, because it always came third, behind Porthcawl and Barry whenever trips were planned from my village. We would either travel to Aberystwyth via Aberaeron, or we would take the longer route, up to Rhayader, and then on through the Elan Valley with all its beautiful reservoirs. I was, initially, disappointed that Aberystwyth did not have a sandy beach, but I always enjoyed my stay and, the walk along the promenade to "kick the bar" at the end, before riding the funicular railway up Constitution Hill and dropping down to Clarach Bay.

Once a year Brynaman Rugby Football Club played Aberystwyth. It was always a "stay-away" fixture in that we stayed for the evening, not over-night. At about 11.30 on a Saturday evening on these Aberystwyth visits, the team bus was to be seen roaming around the town looking for stragglers.

I was guilty one year, posted "missing" along with four others as the bus cruised around looking for any signs of life that the other players recognised. We had become friendly with a few locals, of – how shall I put it – the opposite gender. The evening held promise in the stars that shone across Cardigan Bay, as we walked towards the castle and the pier. Every time I hear the song "Under the Boardwalk" now, I'm reminded of that night, for I hadn't seen Aberystwyth Pier from that angle before … interesting.

ABERSYCHAN AND THE BRITISH CONNECTION

During our college geography course, we had to undertake two surveys. One was in the Vale of Glamorgan, the other in Abersychan.

A friend of mine, Thomas Gilmour Nimrod Jones, or "Spots" by nickname, who'd attended the same grammar school as me, was my companion on this survey. I never found out why he was called "Spots". I don't remember him having bad skin.

We have a photograph of ourselves standing on Abersychan Station during one of our surveying days. The station is no more, neither is the railway line, but the road north to Blaenavon and the famed "Cordell Country", named after Alexander Cordell's earthy novels of the industrial south Wales valleys, passes that way. It was on this survey that I also tracked down the hamlet whose name I first noticed on the destination board of a bus in Cardiff Bus Station – "British" – a strange name for a village that stands on the hill above Abersychan. It compromises just a couple of rows of terraced houses and stands testimony to the industry that went before.

AND NOW FOR A SONG. "I LEFT MY TEETH IN PRIORY GARDENS"

My mother had warned me: 'Now you be careful, you watch out for those Cardiff girls, we don't want any trouble back in this house.'

You can go too far with advice, I think. A

warning becomes curiosity and then moves on to real interest so, I avidly looked out for Cardiff girls for the full three years I was in college but I was never lucky on that score.

My first meeting with some of my fellow Cardiff Training College students was at Astey's café in Cardiff bus station. Looking through the window I wondered where these places were that I saw on the destination boards of the buses – Nantyglo, Abersychan, British, Sebastopol, Oakdale, Cross Keys – they were all new to me. I had seen a few on the map, but not all of them. I got to know the bus routes particularly well, especially the buses running to Heath Park and Cyncoed, where the college was situated.

My 19th birthday involved a bus route. It had been a heavy night, the first away from home. I wasn't feeling one hundred per cent as I stood at the bus stop, so I took a little walk towards the bushes of the Friary Gardens seeking light relief of all kinds. Suddenly there was a shout to say that the bus was coming. I turned swiftly and was about to jump on the bus when someone said,

'Where are your teeth?'

I had lost my two front teeth in an accident some years before. I rushed back to the Priory Gardens, and there they were, on top of a bush, an azalea I think, or was it a hebe? I can't be sure, it was dark and the night had been wearisome. When I returned to the college, I slept like a horse, standing up and gripping the taps at the sink unit for extra stability. That was one of the only two nights that I've been totally drunk. The other was on my Bachelor's night – a week before the wedding, thank heavens. My father put me to bed four times that night and I was still a little uncertain, in vision and longitude, when I met Elaine two days later.

TURN OFF FOR CILYCWM

As a student, I had a summer job two years running with Llandeilo Rural District Council. The first year I was on the "muck gang". The second year, paid a bit more, I was on the "water gang". We gathered in Llandeilo at HQ, and were then allocated duties. A trench at Cilycwm, near Llandovery, was one and we were taken there by van – I think we hold the record for the number of people you can get in a council van. Eight in a small Morris Minor is going some, no Health and Safety then.

It was there, under the guidance of Trevor the foreman from Penygroes, we learned basic common sense, with such gems as:

'Don't go nuts today, boys, 10 yards is a long enough trench for anyone. You want to fill tomorrow with something, so always leave a bit.'

'Now listen, boys, if you're ever digging a trench on a slope, always throw the dirt up-hill, so that you can kick it back in easily on re-fill.'

'If you're ever on the long-armed shovel take your cue from Bob Eak there. I know he's been temporary-full-time for twenty-two years, but he's a trench poet on the long-armed shovel – follow his rhythm, slide, flick, lift, throw, slide, flick, lift throw …

Trevor, the D-Day Dodger war veteran, was a totally balanced man in all senses of the word. On his return, after six years of being away at war, he said, 'I told my wife quietly, it's been a long time, love, we'll ask no questions of each other, we'll start our courting afresh and we'll be fine – and it was.'

Strategic digging relied on local knowledge, not on maps. If we wanted to replace old water pipes, we'd go and find the oldest resident and ask, 'Do you remember the council digging hereabouts years ago? Can you tell us where you think the trench was?'

Under his, or her, guidance, we'd dig a trench gingerly, at right angles to their directions, seeking out the original pipes, usually with 100% success. Except for the once, when Trevor kept shouting, 'Now mind how you go, we don't want a burst pipe today, no slip-ups, it's a Friday. I want to go down the club tonight.'

Ten seconds later, Trevor swung his pick, hit jackpot, and we had a Yellowstone Park geyser on our hands.

PENARTH … THERE'S POSH

"Have chalk will travel."

That was my motivation when I returned to teaching in Wales, and Penarth was one pin on my map of temporary appointments. There are tales told about Penarth that suggest it is rather a snobbish place. I never found it so.

The schools at which I taught in town were always happy, convivial places. The old Penarth Grammar School had two staff rooms – male and female, and the males went out on a Christmas "do" on their own. They did not invite the women. There, druidic circle tradition ruled, to which I and another new teacher were invested at Christmas time, in a pub in Penllyn. The Archdruid was from the maths department and we were all given a Bardic name. At the end of the ceremony we had to kneel before the Archdruid, who had the head of a bear hanging from a ribbon around his neck. Penarth being the Welsh for "head of the bear".

At the end of his eulogy to both of us, he handed the head of the bear towards me and then said, 'You are now known as Roy Ddu, Black Roy from the Black Mountain, and you may now kiss my arth.'

I duly did.

Penarth featured on my life's map some years later. When Elaine and I celebrated our first wedding anniversary it was in a restaurant there on the sea-front. It was a very fine meal and, a fitting occasion but it was the very first time that our bill had crossed the £10 barrier. Although now a married couple, we agreed not to tell our parents about the decadent cost, out of sheer embarrassment and discomfort. Such was my naivety in the setting, that when the head waiter asked me if I wanted some extra vegetables with the steak, I asked him what was available and he suggested that I might wish to try the petits pois.

When the meal arrived I discovered that the

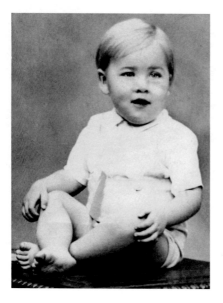

Baby Roy - 1943

Young defender - 1950

James Buses Christmas Party 1949

Brynaman Cinema - early 1950's

Brynaman Carnival 1950 - dressed as an
arab sheik with my father, Ivor Noble

Brynaman Carnival 1952 - I won first prize
as an Indian Prince

Brynaman C.P. School 1953. Mr George was the Head and Miss Williams my teacher

1961 - In Neath with my mum
(wearing my shiny green coat)

1961 - Amman Valley Grammar School Eisteddfod
Roy Noble, Derec Lloyd Morgan, Denzil Jones

1962 - Roy Noble, Trevor Light and Lyn Jones at
the Heath Huts

1964 - College friends, John (Bach) Davies in glasses
and Bob (Robert) Morgan

Aged 20 - President of the Student Union
at Cardiff Training College

Abersychan Station with Gilmour James on a
geography course in 1963

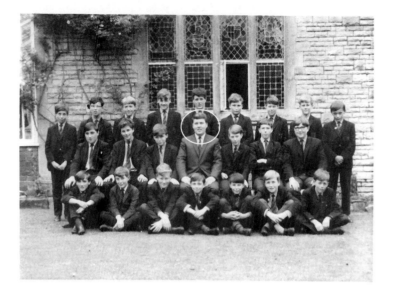

1967 - happy time spent teaching at
Cowbridge Grammar School

1976 - Head teacher at Ysgol Thomas Stephen

Wedding Day - 1st August 1968

1975 - Young family Elaine, Richard and Roy

My father checking out a double decker at
James' Garage, Ammanford

2004 - When I bought a bus -
I owned just the front half!

Promo shot for a TV programme about the
Welsh/English border

Promo shot for "Outside the Box"

S4C surprise challenge - synchronized swimming. I nearly drowned and caught a hell of a cold!

Elaine with Katherine Jenkins

1998 - Pwll Du Head, Gower. Returning to the
spot of our engagement

Receiving the OBE from
HRH Prince Charles - November 2001

Accepted into the Order of Sir John Cymru Wales with the
then Prior, Captain Sir Norman Lloyd Edwards

Accepted into
the Gorsedd of
Bards. National
Eisteddfod -
Cardiff 2008

steak actually came with peas, so when the extra peas came, there were so many that they had to be put on a side plate. That night I was able to go home under my own steam.

SLEEPING AROUND IN COWBRIDGE

AFTER A STINT OF missionary work, teaching in England, I returned to Wales, to take a temporary post, teaching geography at Cowbridge Grammar School, where the headteacher, Mr Idwal Rees, was a strict classics scholar. His rugby pedigree was of the utmost purity, having played in the victorious Welsh team against the All Blacks, of New Zealand, in 1936. I was a little reticent, because I expected the school to be full of Oxbridge trained teachers and wondered whether I would be intimidated. My fears were unfounded and I enjoyed my stay immensely.

As a young buck bachelor, I was often in the company of the two boarding masters of the time: Wyn Oliver, who was in charge of PE, and Iolo Davies, another classics man, who produced the weekly newspaper, "The Bovian". Iolo was a visitor from a time warp, a total eccentric, who wore cavalry twill trousers that ended some six inches from the ground occasionally supported by a tie wrapped around the waist. In their shared study, any gap in the line of books on the bookshelves was filled by a half empty whisky bottle.

Wyn was a small, vibrant West Walian who had sprinted for Wales in the British Empire and

Commonwealth Games, held in Cardiff in 1958. He was about 5 feet 4 inches tall when he was feeling well, but he was explosive and fast as a rugby player, and no boy dared cross him, he was a pocket hand-grenade. When I got to the school, they were still talking about his first day at the school, particularly his self-introduction to the staff. Apparently, he stood at the staffroom door and started counting,

'One, two, three, four ...' until he had counted everyone. 'Right,' he continued, 'a recent survey in the newspapers states that one in every fifteen men is a practising homosexual. There are seventeen in this room, so hands up the queer, so I know where I stand.'

Digs had been arranged for me outside the town, near Crossways, with a very congenial couple, Mr and Mrs Shepherd, who had once been in service in London, so tea and biscuits were served at 7.30 a.m. and my shoes were taken away to be cleaned. Mrs Shepherd's sister, Emily, lived in a caravan at the bottom of the garden, and, such was the service in those digs, I put on two stone in two terms.

Sometimes, the charms of Cowbridge held me until late at night. The boarding masters would arrange that I kip down in the boarding house with the boys. It was a good way of keeping the beds aired.

Character, in all its forms, was the one criteria for appointing the staff, because they had it in spades.

'Don't sit on that chair in the staffroom, Roy,'

was one piece of advice. 'That chair belongs to Darwyn Adams, maths. He likes to sit there because he can supervise his senior class, without leaving the room. He can see them through the window, see, while he has a puff on his pipe.'

The head of history was a published author, although you'd never guess it by his thrifty use of words in school reports, "Hopeless" or "Bemused" or "Non-historic", were examples.

Jeff Alden was head of geography and I worked in his department. He was a lovely man, who became a renowned local historian in Cowbridge. He died, far, far, too young. Sid Harries was another classics man, an ex-rugby player for Swansea, with a glint of mischief in his eye. I remember him, following a staff drinking session in a town pub on our half-day holiday to celebrate St David's Day, jumping on a letter box and eating a daffodil in honour of our saint. He was clearly a man of honour in all things. He told me that he met his wife while she was training to be a nurse. One evening after a date they were late getting back to the nurses' hostel and found it locked. They went in search of an open window, found one, and he helped her to clamber through.

'Roy,' he said, 'In pushing her through the window, I inadvertently placed both my hands on her backside, just to heave you understand – but, after that, I felt I had to marry her.'

An interesting discussion between the caretaker of the Boys' Grammar School and the caretaker of the Girls' High School, in Cowbridge centred on the literary quality of the graffiti in the toilets. I have to report that the caretaker of the Girls' School won hands down. There was a literary imagination and worldly-wise research displayed by the girls that left the Boys' School floundering in basic English and biology.

GIVE ME AN EN-SUITE ANYTIME

I was never in the Scouts. I nearly made the Cubs in Brynaman, when someone set about starting up a troop. We gathered in the Catholic Hall, paid our dues to get everything moving … and didn't hear much after that. I think they're still looking for the fellow who had the money. A pity, I think the Scouts would have hardened me up, taught me survival, and underlined the fact that camping can be for cissies. As it's turned out, tenting has not been in my first division of priorities, pegs and guy-ropes have been beyond the far horizon of my circle of quests.

There was one incident when I 'roughed it'. Llangorse Lake, a place of ancient habitation, but not by ancestors of the Noble tribe I hasten to add, was the site of my one and only experience of camping. I spent the night there with the boys of Cowbridge Grammar School who were on a course, while I was teaching at the school.

My subject, geography, meant I knew where I was, even if I didn't relish it. The groundsheet was certainly waterproof, but it didn't have an air cushion, it was flat, except that it faithfully followed each nook, cranny and corner of a contour line. Consequently, I woke up in the morning as stiff as a board, and with aches in every spot where my body had been at one with nature. Up until then, I thought that the word "earthy" meant something entirely different.

My efforts to get to the ablutions through an early-morning low mist that rendered my ankles missing clearly defined me as a non-Tarzan type. That same day, the PE teacher of the school, Wyn Oliver, a rugged, "I can eat slugs for survival" kind of man, came to join us, so I took my chance, got a doctor's note outlining something exotic, which the town of Cowbridge wouldn't have wanted within its environs and, "God Speed" I was free to go.

THERE'S SAFETY IN NUMBERS, EVEN IN LLANDUDNO

Llandudno's beautiful bay neatly fills the gap between the Great Orme and Little Orme and the shoreline must have impressed and called to any passing Vikings who fancied a bit of a break from rowing.

I saw it at its best on a clear, crisp, star-lit December night, some years after the Viking visitations. The streets of Llandudno were bedecked with Christmas decorations and the coloured lights curved along the bay towards the pier, with the heavy frost given a jewelled shine by the light of the full moon above The Grand Hotel.

I regularly visited as a headteacher, in charge of children on educational visits to north Wales. It was our base for trips to Snowdonia, Llechwedd Slate Caverns, Betws-y-Coed and beyond. It was also our base when we took the Ystradgynlais and District Under-11 rugby side on northern expeditions. One year, we had three Ystradgynlais RFC "Glyns" in support, Glyn, Chairman; Glyn, President; and Glyn, Treasurer. Our group was split between two hotels and, on one strategically-planned evening with the young players safe abed, we shared a drink in one hotel and then accompanied the "Glyns" to theirs. On arrival there, we shared another convivial slurp and they insisted that they accompany us back to our hotel, lest we be mugged or waylaid.

After suitable refreshment in our hostelry, we formed an escort for them on their return journey, recognizing that there is always safety in numbers. If in doubt, form a posse. It's sensible and it is the Welsh committee way of thinking. This inter-hotel "protection and preservation" arrangement went on for three hours.

DON'T CROSS YOUR LEGS UNTIL YOU'RE, AT LEAST, FIFTEEN

Llantwit Major was on my "supply-teaching" route when I first returned to Wales from missionary work teaching in England. I taught at St Illtyd's Primary School, which catered for children at the RAF Station of St Athan. I had the good fortune to stay with one of the characters of the town. Her name was Mrs Mary Pearce and she lived in The Curriers, a disenfranchised pub from the days when bars were either found on a gate or you hit someone with them.

Mrs Pearce provided bed and breakfast and I stayed with her for six months. She was a woman of substance, who took her baths once a week in a tin tub out in the old stable, which had doors on one end and a gaping hole, where a door had once been, in the other. The Curriers is situated in Old Llantwit Major, which is a very picturesque small town. She was hardy and welcoming, providing a breakfast to take a man into a full week's toil and being sure herself, to swig a couple of bottles of Mackeson most evenings, to ward off two threats; an impending chill and, what she considered to be the root of all ills and personal tempest – constipation.

I confess to having had three periods of hypochondria in my life, enjoying all of them. The first one came upon me in Llantwit Major. As I lay in bed of a night, if I wanted to visit the "comfort cabin" – "the little house on the prairie", – "the ty bach", it was at the bottom of the garden. The journey required you to put on six different light switches en-route, before you even got to the back door, and a cold night in January discouraged that kind of expedition anyway but venture you did, for the en-suite was under the bed and, hey, it was 1968, I was years past using one of those.

One particularly trying night, I felt unnaturally cold and I feared that the bed might be a little damp. I had read somewhere, that being very, very cold is one of the most comfortable ways to die and you have to be careful about letting yourself slip away. To protect myself against such inadvertent slippage, I put on a vest under my pyjamas, a tracksuit, a pair of rugby socks, a Dai cap, a pair of gloves and a scarf. I also ripped some pages out of holiday brochures to stick in the window just in case there might be a draught. My Aunty Katie from Port Talbot had warned me about draughts.

'Beware of draughts,' she warned, 'draughts can get at the bones and organs, right through your pores, giving you rheumatism, pleurisy and pneumonia, years before your time.'

Auntie Katy was a Job's comforter. She was a spinster of the Parish on the Cwmafon Road, always dressed in black, loving funerals and with a memory that fanned the family archives from beyond the beyond. She'd had her chances with men. There was a curate from Baglan, apparently, who was very keen, but Katie had duties at home with her unmarried brother Tommy, so the curate got fed up of waiting, and went off with an usherette from the Albert Hall in Swansea.

For a spinster, Katie was worldly wise in the ways of the true and tested remedies. She was full of advice on preventative medicine. She used to say things like, 'If you've washed your hair, don't go to bed for an hour, it will only give you a damp pillow.'

Or, 'Take your vest off at the end of May, put it back on at the end of September, whatever the weather.'

And something very strange, for a spinster, was her remark to me, when I was on my own in my grandmother's kitchen.

'Hey,' she said, 'Roy, being that you are a boy don't cross your legs until you're at least fifteen.'

Thinking back, I wish I'd listened to her.

Her words returned to me in Llantwit Major. After the draught, the imaginary damp bed and the extreme cold. I wondered whether my extra lagging had been enough. Over the next few weeks, I began to have aches and pains all over the place, so I visited the doctor.

It was the first time I encountered an appointment system, because, in Brynaman, with Dr Warner, it had been a simple queuing system, with Mondays being a very popular day. Mondays were "Doctor's Paper Days" when men could get signed off work for the week. There were regulars on Mondays, well known to the doctor, and if they didn't turn up, the Doctor really thought they were ill.

The doctor in Llantwit Major checked me over and couldn't find anything wrong at all.

'Now, listen,' he said. 'You've too many pains in too many places for it to be serious. It might be psychoneurosis.'

"Psychoneurosis" – big word; that was good enough for me.

'Now,' he continued, 'is there anything on your mind, anything bothering you at all, anything out of the ordinary that's filling your mind, playing on your thoughts?'

'Not really,' I replied. 'No worries, no bother. I'm coping with the plans for the wedding all right.'

'Ah-ha! Marriage, eh, there we have it, your sea-change of life. Your mind is preparing for that, and your body is trying to keep up with your mind. Let me tell you now, I've been there, done it, got the certificate – I can assure you, that once your marriage has taken place, your aches and pains will be gone, your mind will be distracted, it will be too busy dealing with other problems."

PSSST ... KNOW A COUNCILLOR?

"TRANSPARENCY", NOW THERE'S AN "in" word these days. All official dealings and doings must be open to scrutiny, fully transparent.

Transparency isn't new, of course. We knew it as a side-effect of many of the official "goings on" and decision-making years ago; in fact, it was sometimes so transparent, we could see right through it from miles away.

Take local authority appointments, where each application form had a line at the bottom of the first page stating "Canvassing of local authority members will disqualify the candidate". What a load of fiction that was; in some counties, canvassing seemed second only to mixed farming or heavy industry output as a way of life.

Teaching appointments were an example of local authority members becoming "local squires" of influence. Indeed, headship appointments became minefields of uncertainty.

When Elaine and I were due to marry, we were both interviewed for teaching jobs in the Caerffili & Gelligaer Division of Glamorganshire. All was done alphabetically, so, in the list of candidates, Elaine, as an "Evans" was way higher than myself as a "Noble". When it came to my turn, a benign, jocular councillor on the panel said, 'Mr Chairman, remember now, if you appoint Noble, number twelve, you must appoint Evans, number five, because they are – romantically inclined.'

What a marvellous man, he knew that lust and liability can be comfortable bed-fellows. No canvassing had been done, yet we were both duly appointed.

My first headship interview was rather bizarre. It must have been market day in Brecon, for thirty councillors sat on the appointing panel in Breconshire County Hall. The ancient county of Breconshire was due to be amalgamated into the new county of Powys, so, as it transpired, Powys and I started together, me as a head, and Powys as a county.

As the candidates, myself included, waited in the designated room, the large appointing panel walked through into the interview chamber. Quite a few of them were nodding to two of the candidates, and I thought to myself, aye aye, two of those boys have been canvassing the councillors for this post. I've no chance. I'm here just as cannon fodder.

Interviews over, shock of shocks, I was recalled to the chamber and offered the post. Six months later, the sitting local authority member, for the area in which the school was situated, called to see me.

'I've got to tell you,' he said, 'I didn't vote for you at first, because you hadn't been to see me. You hadn't canvassed me, so I didn't know who the hell you were. You did put up a good show in the council chamber, mind, but we had some trouble that day. Two of the other candidates had canvassed so heavily that we couldn't get a majority for either, fifteen votes each, so we had a recount – fifteen each again. In the end, the Chairman suggested a compromise, so we all voted for you.'

My second headship appointment, some seven years after the first, involved a "long shortlist" and a "short shortlist" system. It was at Powys HQ, the County Hall in Llandrindod Wells. Those doing well at the morning's "long shortlist", were invited to the reduced number, "short shortlist", in the afternoon.

At lunchtime, for natural relief after the adrenalin rush, I visited the "gentlemen's comfort zone" – the "Gents". In the conveniences was a cohort of councillors, chatting quietly. They saw me enter, fell totally silent, and all left except one. I don't want to be graphic, but there I was, standing in one trough, with a senior councillor in the next one. As we stood there about our business and staring at the tiles, he suddenly said, 'You did well this morning, play your cards right this afternoon and you're in.'

A surge of confidence welled within me but, bearing in mind where we were and what we were doing, I resisted the temptation to shake his hand there and then. I merely said, 'Thank you very much. But there's a strong candidate from Birmingham against me in the "short shortlist" this afternoon.'

'Oh, don't worry about him,' he said. 'He was too strong, he was a complication in the "grand plan" so we dropped him this morning.'

The truth, as it became clear some days later, was that the Local Authority wanted to close the neighbouring village school to mine at Ystradfellte, and the redundant headteacher there would get my headship, if I was promoted elsewhere ... out of the way. It all came to pass. Their chess game was complete, everything was, as the councillor proclaimed, "Hunky dory".

Mind you, to be fair, in that Local Authority you were at least given five questions at the interview and all the time in the world to answer. I've known some local authorities, in those days, who only allowed two questions and you were given just five minutes on a stopwatch, to answer both.

I heard of one candidate who was so traumatised by the procedure she failed to say a word at interview but still got the job. I suppose that in failing to say anything, she at least didn't say anything wrong. Her canvassing must have been effectively strategic, so you couldn't argue that she was weak on interpersonal and communication skills, but, as a headteacher, who knows?

I also heard a tale of one councillor in a west Wales local authority, telling a canvassing candidate, 'The job's yours, boy. I haven't had a candidate in the field for two years, so the other members owe me 52 votes, you'll walk it.'

Tales abound, even of "money changing hands" or favours promised in exchange for teaching headships. I never knew of anything like that, and stories, once they get on the road, tend to travel miles, heading towards urban myths.

"Pssst, know a councillor?" It was the definitive professional first step to success.

Of course, knowing a councillor, or at least getting his vote, could be of real benefit in many social fields beyond teaching and other local authority appointments. Take "council houses" for instance. Being put on "the list", and actually getting a council house, was the ambition of many young couples, especially in the late 1940s and into the 1950s.

A young married couple's first "home", was very often the bride's parents' front room. After a honeymoon in a guest house, in Sussex Gardens, Paddington, or somewhere similar if they could afford it, they'd come home and set up "house" in their parents' parlour. Most terraced houses were not blessed with "wall to wall" privacy, the walls being so thin, in some cases, that you could hear someone "change their mind" from two doors away.

Getting "on the list" for a council house was the thing. Knowing a councillor, or knowing someone who was a friend of a councillor, or even related to one, was a great advantage. You could quietly move "up the list". A member's vote or effort on your behalf often had a leapfrogging effect and you could go from number twenty-four to number eight in priority with no trouble at all.

Oh yes, "Pssst … do you know a councillor?" was a hissed question that very often took you on the first step to success and fulfilment, professional or personal.

Princes in their parishes, kings in their corners … straight after Election Day anyway.

THE BLACK POOL WITH HIDDEN DEPTHS

THE LAZY, HAZY, CRAZY days of summer often saw me, with the boys, at Pwll Du Uchaf and Pwll Du Isaf, the Upper and Lower Black Pools, on the Garw River, on the mountain moorland above Brynaman. They were joyous days of jumping, splashing and sliding into the deep water. Showing off meant pretending that you could swim, making sure that you could get one foot on the floor as you went. Showing off could only be done at the shallow edges. No one worried about polluted water, even though there might have been a dead sheep higher upstream. A picnic was just one round of sandwiches and bottle of water. I don't think biscuits had been invented in those early days of the 1950s, I certainly didn't see many about, in company or in our pantry.

It's funny how life's path weaves, turns, and sometimes returns to a distant memory by touching something new. It happened on New Year's Day, 1967. Elaine and I had decided to get engaged on that day. I figured that, with anniversaries, you should choose a date that will be easy to remember. That's why we married on August 1st 1968.

I can easily remember the day in those

important months, so if I can work out the year, I'm laughing. Mind you, perhaps I'm doing myself down because I can remember the date of our meeting in college. It was the third Wednesday in January, 1964 during my last year in college, her first year. I was the Student Union President – I think she went for the position. Oh boy, did I make use of the newly agreed cross gender 'visiting' arrangements in college. I well recall that killer invitation to Elaine. It was drawn up from the deep recesses of my brain's creative wing.

'Do you fancy a coffee?'

Thank God, she's been "fancying coffee" for quite a few years now.

On that New Year's Day of '67, we headed out from my home, to, I knew not where. I wanted somewhere special to leap out at me as I drove. For some reason, we were guided towards the Gower peninsular, and as we came round a corner near Pennard leading to Southgate, there it was – a sign pointing to Pwll Du Bay. "Pwll Du," I thought. It's a sign – more than a road-sign. A direction turn for life. If you haven't been to Pwll Du Bay, why not? It's quiet, off the beaten track, a secluded, serenely beautiful bay, and for a romantic backdrop, perfect.

I did the whole bit, down on one knee, no complicated responses I'm glad to say, so, a first step to over forty years so far. We rounded it all off with a Sunday roast at the Caswell Bay Hotel, no longer there, sadly. We had beef – well done, as is my wont.

ILLEGALLY MARRIED, THE DEACONS WOULDN'T LIKE IT

Gwawr Chapel at Godreaman, Aberdare, is the chapel where Elaine worshipped and where we married in 1968. When the original Gwawr Chapel was demolished as unsafe, the Welsh Baptist members took over the vacant Hebron Chapel and re-named it. The problem was that no one remembered to re-register it as a place for marriages. When that realisation dawned on us a week before the wedding, there were some fast and frantic rearrangements made with the registrar. Good heavens! Our marriage was almost illegal, and that would never have done. After all, Elaine's father had been a deacon at Gwawr.

Prior to our wedding, I had become a regular member at Gwawr and, while listening to one or two visiting ministers, I became convinced that there should be a question and answer session after each sermon. Just because a statement comes from a pulpit, doesn't mean that it was rubber-stamped by the Almighty prior to release. One young, trainee, minister even suggested that the Aberfan tragedy, where so many children and adults were killed by a sliding coal tip, was probably some kind of penance for an earlier sin. His closing prayer was drowned out by my inner fervent hope that he would fail his finals dismally and that he'd end up in some burdensome secular, soul-searing job, one which would cause him sleepless nights.

The Minister of Gwawr was the Rev Arfon Jones, who with his wife, Enyd, and children,

Deiniol and Eiri, became lifelong and valued family friends. Arfon, as many ministers do, suggested diplomatically to the guests, that, in our wedding, confetti should be thrown at the bottom of the chapel steps but not, if possible, near the chapel door, where it might blow in. He had reckoned without my Sicilian uncle, Isidoro Viola. He was very excitable and a man moved by the moment. He wasn't quite out of the chapel pew when he started. His confetti, taken by the breeze, reached the deacons' "big seat" just below the pulpit.

Isidoro had been a prisoner of war, caught in the Sahara by the Desert Rats and, ended up working on a farm in Cwmgors when he met, and married, my Aunty Katie. They had five children in five years; then he gave up Catholicism. I was downstairs, in my grandmother's house, when they had their fourth, so was Isidoro. The midwife came down and when he offered to help, she gave him a steely look of "Stay there; it's all your fault anyway."

I liked Isidoro very much, although we all called him Viola, his surname. He worked in "open-cast" mining for years, way beyond retirement age, because his papers were a little wayward and no one was quite sure of his age. He knew, but he kept quiet about it because he loved working. He was of good Sicilian stock, two of his brothers rising to become town clerks on the island. He also kept saying that Mussolini was a "good guy" for southern Italy, making all the trains and water taps run regularly and, keeping the Mafia indoors, until he had ideas of becoming Caesar.

Then it all went pear-shaped or, I suppose, olive-shaped in Italy.

It's a funny thing though, for all his years in this country, he had two continuing weaknesses. His accent remained very Sicilian and, on his motor-bike, he thought red lights were a challenge. Perhaps he was colour blind.

NOW COME ON, IS IT A PARLOUR, OR BEDROOM?

Elaine and I spent our wedding night at the Park Hotel, Cardiff, in the room above the Scholl shop in Queen Street. The room cost £6, but they billed it as 120 shillings for some reason, which was an extraordinary amount to pay in 1968. Good grief, the entire honeymoon was only costing £49 each, flight and full board in Cala Bona, Majorca included.

Mind you, this room, above the Scholl Shoe Shop, did have a three-piece suite in it, which was something new for us, a front room and bedroom combined. Bit of a waste I thought at the time. The Scholl shop is no more, I think "La Baguette" is there now, and Queen Street is pedestrianised, unlike 1968, when traffic was in full noisy flow, except for the trolley buses, which were lethally quiet. The noise kept us awake all night.

We stayed there just the one night, our wedding night. Our honeymoon flight was due out on the Friday, but someone had told me that getting married on a Friday was unlucky in Wales. I don't know if it's true or not, but we opted for the

Thursday, just in case. Being a romantic devil, I decided we should go rowing on Roath Park Lake – which totally knackered me.

COME FLY WITH ME

He didn't look like a pilot; he was wearing a Dai flat cap, a rough jumper and a pair of black Wellington boots. I had entered a newspaper competition, seeking a prize of flying lessons. You paid for a trial appraisal and the instructor gauged which candidate showed most promise.

I'd expected somebody flash wearing a leather jacket, white scarf with goggles thrown back nonchalantly on to his leather helmet. Instead, I was confronted by Worzel Gummidge. After starting up, he allowed me to taxi the aircraft down the runway.

All right, I wasn't very good, weaving from side to side as if checking all parts of the concrete for pot-holes, but, once in the air, I thought, "I'll be in my oils."

Not at all, once we were airborne, he kept shouting,

'Don't touch anything – leave it alone – I'll do it.'

How they could choose a candidate with best potential, to win the prize, is still beyond me. It must have been one of those "Welsh" jobs, already marked out for someone "in the know" or who knew someone of influence, you know what it was like.

Cardiff Airport was the scene of my first,

proper, airliner experience. I had been up in an RAF Hastings when I was a member of the Royal Observer Corps. I was disorientated then, because all the seats were "back to front". We all had our backs to the pilot. It was a quick flip above Cardiff. Incidentally, our Observer Corps base was in Gwaun Cae Gurwen and we were part of 13 Group, based at Carmarthen. I still know where the GCG Bunker is, but I'm sworn to secrecy. That information is for another time and place ... in this book.

So to my first airliner out of Cardiff, a Cambrian Airways Vickers Viscount. I still have a large model of the aeroplane at home, as a piece of romantic nostalgia. I'm soft like that. Following our marriage, Elaine and I were due to fly to Majorca for our honeymoon. I didn't realise at the time that the seat tickets were not numbered so you could sit where you liked on the aircraft, and being a gentleman, I allowed most of the people to get on the flight before me. Consequently, I found myself going on honeymoon, sitting four rows away from my bride. Furthermore, after taxi-ing to the runway, it was found that the door was not securely closed. Elaine was a fearful flier and there was no one to hold her hand on the second day of marriage.

Where was her bold and protective prince? Four rows behind her, that's where. I made up my mind that on the return journey, things would be different. Come hell or high water, we would be sitting together.

A fortnight later at Palma Airport, waiting for

the return flight, we sat near the door so that when the flight number was called we would be near the front of the queue, and so it proved to be. As we were led across the tarmac by an air-hostess, towards the waiting Viscount, we were about four couples from the front. Suddenly, a man from Bargoed began to run from the back of the queue. He had a sombrero on his head and was carrying a stuffed donkey, along with two large pieces of hand luggage. He had decided that he wanted a good seat on the plane, so he'd broken into a gallop. One or two others decided that it wasn't such a bad idea, and they began sprinting as well. The queue broke up. It was like a rush of refugees trying to get on the last flight out of some desperate country.

I could see out of the corner of my eye into the Terminal Building where crowds of people were staring at us from the large windows and, probably wondering, "Who are those people, what are they running from, and is Wales such a Valhalla of attraction that they're all fighting to be the first to get there?"

The air-hostess stood at the foot of the steps shouting, 'Back, back, you can't get on – order please, there's room for all.'

Her pleas were cast aside. We went up the steps three abreast, one or two of the larger types overhanging the sides with their stomachs. I must have been twentieth or twenty-first on to the aircraft, but I am proud to say I managed to sit next to my new wife all the way home, and holding hands.

ABERDARE SNAKES AND OTHER WILDLIFE IN THE CYNON VALLEY

I LIVE IN ABERDARE because of a woman … Elaine. Ah, the power of attraction in lust and love. Although my roots are further west in Brynaman, the Cynon Valley has now become my home. The people who live there are called Aberdare Snakes. There are many stories given as to the origin of the name, but I believe it goes back to a strike by miners in the early 20th century, when the Aberdare region did not come out in support. I am always open to other suggestions, of course, if someone knows better.

I remember very well the first occasion I came to the Valley. I travelled up from Cardiff on a Red and White bus to meet Elaine's parents for the first time. It was a Sunday and I was due there for "Sunday dinner". I asked the bus driver to put me off at Aberaman Bridge. I have to say that I was very impressed with the house because they had a bathroom indoors and an automatic washing machine as well. Our en-suite at home in Brynaman hung on a nail outside the back door. It was near the semi-detached toilets between our house and the Price's next door.

My mother didn't have an automatic washing

machine for years, nor did she have a cooker. For some illogical reason, I think she thought that all of that smacked of "cheating" in the household chores. All her cooking was done in the oven at the side of the coal fire grate, but she eventually condescended to have a washing machine which had a mangle attached to it to squeeze the water from the clothes.

Aberdare has been good to me and I have enjoyed my life here. Elaine and I have many friends and they certainly keep my feet on the ground. Broadcasting, after all, is just a job, and there can be no airs and graces in this area. I remember in my early days of broadcasting going into a pub in Aberdare and being asked by one of the locals, 'Was it you on the radio this morning, Roy?'

My chest swelled a little and I answered, 'Yes, it was.'

'Wasn't much bloody good, was it?' he said.

Thinking about his comments later, I promised myself that, if ego ever reared its head, it should be dismantled immediately by myself, before anyone else, rightly, showed it its place. Those who know me only too well wouldn't have it any other way.

SHEEPLESS, NOT IN SEATTLE BUT IN MOST VALLEY VILLAGES

I was once jealous of the sheep you see in most rural areas of Wales. Compared to the indigenous Nelson or Glamorgan sheep you get in the valleys, they are tidy sheep – controlled sheep, "staying in fields" sheep. The valleys' woolly roamer is an in-bred Gulliver – always travelling.

That jealousy has turned to nostalgia, because you don't seem to see as many these days. Oh, they're still on the roads all right, roving about but not to be seen in housing estates as they once were. When Elaine and I lived in our first estate house – estates were the thing then, with sapele doors, wall-to-wall carpet, and G-Plan furniture if you were feeling flush; sheep were part of the scene.

If you think of that old film, *Elephant Walk*, where a bungalow had been built across an ancient elephant track and, when the innate call was upon them, they walked right through the transgressing bungalow's lounge and bedroom, then our valley sheep were something similar, if not quite so dramatic.

You see, before the Industrial Revolution and, the rapid urbanisation of the valleys, sheep had free roaming rights over this patch of Wales. Even when the iron and the coal came, the Nelson and Glamorgan sheep adjusted to developments. Ewes taught their lambs when "dust-bin" days were. – Mondays and Thursdays on our estate, so they came to forage for morsels not usually found in the natural flora of south Wales.

As we lay in bed at night Elaine and I came to recognise the "regulars" in the flock by their bleats, as they wandered up the street. Sometimes, you'd hear a lamb's high, urgent bleating, because he'd mislaid his mam. Then, twenty minutes later, the deeper bleat, of the mam looking for her lamb. Concern crept in for their welfare too, especially for that, clearly very mature, ewe, that had a nasty bronchial cough. Patience waned when your dustbin was tipped over, for the sheep learned to take the lid off the old aluminium bins. The advanced part of the course they'd been on was the "rolling over the cattle grid" certificate. The first ewe to do that must be holding a Nobel Prize in sheep tactics, along with a highly commended badge for realising that, in wintertime, "cat's eyes" on roads are a great source of salt after the gritters have been out.

Someone once told me that a sheep will not jump over a fence or wall if it's not sure of the ground on the other side. No one has told the Glamorgan sheep that, for I've seen several Zebedees bounce over in the vertical. You have to be careful of "country tales" of that kind.

I had the opportunity to test deeply held agricultural lore and wisdom when I worked one summer as a student with Llandeilo Rural District Council. We were in a trench in a field, outside Talley near Llandeilo, laying a new water main to a cottage occupied by two Polish men, who had not been able to go back to their homeland after the war.

Gareth, another student, suddenly asked, 'Can you hear thunder?'

It was a lovely day, so we poked our heads above the trench, and there it was – a bull, charging down the field, straight for us.

I'd read somewhere that bulls have two weaknesses you should bear in mind, if you are threatened. One, they are colour-blind, so it's the bull-fighter's swaying cape that bothers the bull, not the colour. Academic knowledge outside Llandeilo, I know, but there we go. The second supposed weakness was of more immediate interest. Bulls can't run down hill. The tonnage heading for us, in that field, was clearly educationally disadvantaged; he didn't know that bit about downhill sprinting being a "no-go" athletic event for heavy male bovians.

Gareth and I were out of that trench like my Auntie Marged out of a scalding hot bath – not stylish, but swift. We reached the field gate in a dead heat, he climbed over, but I, finding prowess from a primeval past, went over it without bending my body, a mighty bound. It was another version of the innovative Fosbury flop in international high-jumping, only I was totally vertical – isn't it always the case, no one has a camera when you need it.

Back in the woolly world, I also thought that sheep don't like daffodils. Our visitors tried them anyway and then spat them out. If your wrought-iron gate was not of "heavy-duty" metal, the ewes would lift them off their hinges and walk through the estate with the gates wrapped around their necks.

The women of the flock were the foragers; I never saw a ram make the effort. Typical, I suppose. Nowadays, there aren't as many, rams, ewes or lambs about. They are still to be seen on roadsides, especially in moorland and open pastures. Coming over the Bwlch, above Treorci, some years ago, I stopped in a lay-by where the ice-cream van is sited. It was late March, but it was snowing, and the trade at the van was sparse. I had never had ice-cream in falling snow, so I went over to get my ice-cream wafer, where I found myself in a queue, the lady in the van was feeding cornets to a few valley sheep. They were clearly, from their dishevelled state, the SAS section of their flock, having lost great clumps of wool from their backs after crawling through wire fencing.

Valley sheep, a breed of their own. I once asked Dai Llanilar, a farmer renowned for his S4C farming television programme "Cefn Gwlad" for his observations on this unique branch of the sheep tribes.

'Roy bach,' he answered, 'the Nelson or Glamorgan sheep is a renegade. A breed of independent movement and thought. A free spirit. The only way you can control them is in a freezer – and even then, you'd have to lock it.'

THE WOMEN'S INSTITUTE TOO CLOSE FOR COMFORT

The WI always fills my thoughts at Margam Park. If I'm honest, I confess to being a WI groupie. I've spoken to so many WI Groups that I must be an Honorary Member, gender-bending permitting. I am a fan.

Margam Park is a beautiful oasis east of industrial Port Talbot. It is always a pleasure to visit and appreciate the layers of history that are encompassed in the Abbey, the fine house, the roaming deer, the Orangery and the ancient ruins on the hill.

My abiding "smile maker" of recall involves the WI in this magnificent setting. A rally had been organized by the Women's Institute and in kindness they'd invited Elaine and myself. I was to officially open the day. As we drove into the park, I found the designated parking spot, stopped, and was immediately hit from the rear by another car. Great embarrassment – it turned out to be the WI Driver of the year.

A LEAP OF FAITH

IT WAS ON JANUARY 25th 1926 that he arrived in Canada, on the SS *Montcalm* as a young man pushing twenty.

Ivor Henry Noble, my father, had taken a £10 emigration scheme opportunity and left Penybank, Ammanford, where the family then lived, for a life in British Columbia.

I still have a photograph of him at home, every inch a cowboy, all the way up to his eyebrows. On horseback, with stubble on his chin and a cigarette in his mouth, he looked the part, until you came to the flat "Dai Cap" on his head.

After a few years, the depression hit Canada, so he returned home, eventually met my mother, and here I am.

My father was a quiet, benign, lovely man who had burned all the adventure he ever needed in that one, long journey to Canada. That became all too clear every Bank Holiday even when my parents had a car, when my mother, Sarah Hannah – known throughout her life as Sadie, stood at the window, sighing heavily, wanting a little spin in the Ford Anglia. But he didn't want to go anywhere. I didn't like those tense Bank Holidays. It was eased when I passed my test, and I could take my mother for a ride.

That burned-up adventure, leading to a side-effect of extreme reticence, must have been passed on to me. I was never one to make a leap of faith. I mean, there are dreamers and "doers" and the "doers" are the ones who put the rivets in dreams so they come to fruition. I was never great at welding.

BIGGLES

Perhaps I put myself down too readily, because there have been occasions where I've stepped outside myself, so far outside that I was standing on a different latitude and longitude.

Ever since I'd read the "Eagle" comic, with tales of "Dan Dare, pilot of the future", I wanted to be an RAF pilot. The chance came when I'd been teaching just two years. I applied for RAF aircrew selection at Biggin Hill Airfield, in Kent. I gave up my first teaching post, at Bath, to clear the decks for my intended new career.

Selection at Biggin Hill was over four days. The first medical set the tone. There were forty candidates and, by the law of averages, not everyone was able to provide a specimen at the drop of a hat, or trousers. One candidate was so desperate, that another, out of pity said, 'Oh for heaven's sake, have some of mine.'

And he did.

Throughout each day, after subsequent tests in aptitude, maths, basic logic and so on, a tannoyed voice would announce, 'Mr Smith, please go to room 16.'

Room 16 was "the chop room", where men were told that they had failed a test and there was no point in staying.

I was still there at the end of Day 3. My hopes were "sky blue"-high, until, on Day 4, the tannoyed voice cut me to the core with, 'Mr Noble, go to room 16.'

I was chopped.

My problem was honesty. I had put down on my medical form – in answer to the question "Do you have any allergies?" – hay fever.

'We can't have pilots sneezing,' said the Squadron Leader.

'I'll serve in cold climates then,' I replied weakly.

'We have no such climate left in the Commonwealth,' he countered.

I was out. I remember, on my return, stepping on to the platform at Paddington Station with my "hangdog" look down to Welsh corgi level. Furthermore, I'd left my pyjamas at Biggin Hill. New ones, brown with beige piping. I hope some pilot or navigator wore them, in comfort and safety.

SCHOOL, LET ME OUT OF HERE

Three years of teaching, that's all it had taken to unsettle the mind. I had begun to wonder, "There must be life outside teaching." I'd gone to school at four years of age, left school at eighteen and, at twenty-one, I was back in school. What was out there, beyond the chalk dust, the playground duty and those black school railings?

The *Western Mail* job advertisement page provided a glimpse one week. "Vacancy – Plant Manager of a Concrete Company required, £1,005 and a car."

In 1967 this was the stuff of dreams and decadence. I applied and received an invitation for an interview.

Are there forces at large, beyond our control, that decide our destiny? There must be. For on my journey to the interview I was a victim to unreasonable occurrences, breeze blocks thrown in my path, delay and damage.

The M4 Motorway had not been built, so I was heading east, to my "concrete" future, on the A48, when, in the village of Pyle, I had, not one, but two punctures. A pair of tyres, flat as a smoothing iron.

With help, I managed to replace one and partially inflate the other, and I tramped to the kiosk on Pyle Square, to telephone my excuses and give advanced warning of my grease-bedecked state. The interview panel said they'd wait. I never got there.

As I turned to open the telephone kiosk door a man was standing there, in a brown mackintosh and black beret, with eyes close together and a friendly, if distant, smile upon his face. He wouldn't let me out. He kept leaning heavily on the door. No amount of cajoling, threatening, pushing, shoving, swearing, shouting for help would shift him. I was in there for twenty minutes. On finally getting out, in an utterly dishevelled state, I went home, on three and a half tyres.

I don't know if my kiosk assailant was the village idiot in Pyle, or whether they have a rota for idiots there. Or perhaps he was a visitor from another village, out for the day. Whoever he was, I was convinced he'd been sent by some higher being, an angel, dressed for the weather, to stop me from making a mistake. Concrete Plant at £1,005 a year, plus a car, was not for me. Fate and the man in the mac had seen to that.

A FOOT IN THE BBC DOOR

My father, after his initial escapades in Canada, coal-mining and bus-driving, had, evangelically, converted to the "safe job" philosophy: "Get 40 years in and a wristwatch at the end of it, that's what you want." Any attempt by me to counter that and step outside the norm of "good job and pension" would have meant a lunge at my lapels and a close query from Dad as to "What the hell are you doing?"

Dad had passed on before the *Western Mail* threw up a new temptation. By this time, it was more of a gamble. I was a headteacher and back in college, on a sabbatical for a year, seeking out a degree. Yet, there it was, a job advertisement, "BBC Wales requires a Radio Presenter: details below."

I read and re-read the advert. It didn't seem to have a clear job description at all. 'This is a Welsh job,' I thought. 'A job they've got to advertise because it's a public appointment, but it must be earmarked for someone who knows someone, who's related to someone on an influential committee, no chance there then.'

In a fit of rebellion, I decided to try a different tack, for, inside me, a voice was saying, "Noble, you can do this." Childishly, I started to send BBC Wales a blank piece of paper, every day, with just two words on it: Roy Noble.

This went on for two months and by this time I was adding big words from Roget's Thesaurus to describe this boy from Aberdare, nee Brynaman, that they were missing out on. Then I started including my telephone number and cutting out photographs of good looking men from magazines, and writing on them, "This is me in Acapulco", or "This is me at the Queen's Garden Party".

The Head of Programmes was Ms Teleri Bevan and, with cajoling from Madeleine, her secretary, 'You must see this nut – there's something about him', I was invited to BBC HQ, the famed Taff Mahal. God bless them both.

Once there, I was told that the advertised job had fallen, by default, because of cutbacks, but several hundred had applied.

They invited me to have a look around and the senior producer on the AM programme, David Nicholas, known as Dai Nick, invited me to do temporary research work for them, during my school holidays. My foot wasn't exactly in the door but my big toe was.

The presenter was Chris Stuart, a talented and lovely man, and it was he who gave me my first interview. The subject was "Course rugby refereeing", which I was doing at the time.

Gradually I developed from there to writing

and presenting 'Letter from Aberdare' once a week; the scenario being the musings of five men who met in their local Club and Institute every Sunday morning. They were Cec of Cemetery Road, Herbert "Pacemaker" Lewis, Isi Bevan, Vince Evans and Conshie Davies – a club inner sanctum of high IQ, if taken as a group combined total. Their deliberations and debates covered a quilt of subjects, some more colourful than others, ranging from local gossip to national crisis and world-wide news.

Indeed, just like barbers and taxi drivers, if the government of the day had tapped into their intellect and common sense, then this country would not have had any international problems by high noon on any Sunday.

INTELLECTUALLY CHALLENGED

My BBC flirtation was on a part-time basis, being that I was still a headteacher at the time. As the years passed, so the relationship grew and, in 1984, I was invited to join BBC Wales full-time. I'm not a decisive man and I couldn't make a decision. My father's words kept coming back to me, "A secure job, that's what you want, 40 years, a pension and a pocket watch at the end of it".

Fate took a hand and helped me out. Fate, they say, is what happens to you, but destiny is what you do with what happens to you, but, now and again, you've got to put your head above the parapet, so that destiny can see you. Did I jump, or was I pushed?

Well, some six months after the BBC's initial offer of a freelance presenter's position, I was visited by two of Her Majesty's Inspectors of Schools. I had already won two scholarships to visit schools in Germany and America to undertake comparative education studies and I was on one or two influential committees for my employing local authority. The inspectors were there to suggest that I might be interested in a vacant post of Primary Schools Inspector at the Welsh Office.

Of course I was interested, and, naively perhaps, I thought I had a good chance. After all, two inspectors of schools had gone out of their way to point me towards the vacancy. Confidence coursed to all the commonwealth regions of the Noble mind and body, I really fancied the royal seal on my briefcase.

Confidence, of course, is that strong feeling you get just before you fall flat on your face. I applied, heard nothing and was not chosen as one of the candidates invited for interview. My mood was black, my depression deep, but it was all put into context some weeks later. On making a few tentative enquires, I was told that Welsh Office officials had approached my employing Local Authority, seeking "off the record" references about this fellow Roy Noble. A senior officer at the County had responded with, 'Oh no. Have you heard the style of his weekly broadcast? Very light-hearted, very frivolous, oh no, his intellect is clearly not up to the mark required of an inspector of schools.'

I heard of that assessment in a hotel room in

Seattle, while on the American Scholarship tour. I looked out of the bedroom window, straight at the distant Mount St Helen's which had blown its backside off just a year before in a volcanic explosion. 'Noble bach,' I thought, 'you clearly haven't made an impression in some corners of County Hall, even though you've been a headmaster of two schools.'

I should have taken a hint some years previously when, as headmaster of my first school, someone who wanted to contact me had telephoned County Hall and asked,

'Have you got a headmaster named Noble in the county?'

The reply was, 'No, we don't. We did have, but he's passed away I'm afraid.'

I looked at Mount St Helen's again, minus its backside, and D-Day crept up on me. The BBC it was then. Whoever that County Hall education senior official was who had doubts about my intellect, he did me a favour really, he pulled my destiny lever and set me off and, so far, fate has been very kind indeed.

With Teleri Bevan's encouragement and with the support of Megan Emery as Editor of Radio Wales and some marvellous team members, my big toe in the door became a foot. It's not a big foot, just size 7 when I'm feeling well, but it is high instep and very broad-fitting, so I take encouragement from that.

ANY PROBLEM ... RING ARTHUR

YSTRADFELLTE IS RENOWNED FOR its river and waterfall scenery and is an area of quite magnificent walks and picturesque views, with the Sarn Helen Roman Road skirting the north of the village. Pontneddfechan further down in an appendix of the county of Powys, has a charm of its own, at the head of the Neath Valley, and there are fine vistas as you look down the valley itself and across to the high ridge that marks the northern edge of the south Wales coalfield, above Rhigos.

Graig Dinas, "Dinas Rock", is part of the village and it is said that there is a hidden, secret cave at the base of the cliff face where King Arthur and his knights sleep. If ever Wales is threatened, then someone will find the cave, ring the bell that hangs at its entrance, and Arthur and his warriors will awake, leap to their feet and charge out to save us all. I've searched avidly for this cave. No joy so far but, if ever we do have a major problem, I'll take a bus-load of diviners and geologists down there for a blitzkrieg of an expedition. Even then, with my luck I'd ring Arthur's bell and get an engaged tone.

I was headteacher of Ysgol Thomas Stephens in Pontneddfechan, for seven years, and enjoyed my time there immensely. It only had some 50 pupils, varying from year to year. The school was sited opposite the Glynneath Golf Club, the president of the club being the famed Max Boyce, whom I'm pleased to call a good friend. My executive duties as a headteacher would, on occasion, stretch a measure beyond normal educational criteria.

The odd day would see me shooting past the golf club in my car, chasing the dinner van, on my way to Ystradfellte School. Our school canteen provided Ystradfellte School with all meals. Very often the custard or gravy was left behind and, I had to take it up in the boot of my car. I rarely caught the van, so the custard often arrived quite a bit later than the pudding. And the gravy, if it made it at all, had a crust on it. It was a lovely road to journey on though, with spectacular views south to the south Wales valleys' ridges and north to the Brecon Beacons.

The eight miles there and back firmly cooled the mind and set the blood pressure at manageable elevations. The trip was therapeutic. Well, you can't rush headlong along curving and dipping country lanes when you've gravy or custard in the boot of your car.

They were happy days in Ysgol Thomas Stephens, with supportive staff and lovely parents. The one black mark was the day I was on a course, and the staff allowed the school to be used by a Spiritual Medium in school time. Well, she was in the village; many of the locals were keen to attend but, the question of a venue had been overlooked, so why not the school hall? When I heard about it, I had a fit, thank heavens no one reported us to the

Local Authority

I thought it a good idea, one day, to hold a pets' morning in school. Most children brought their usual domestic pets, cats, dogs, a hamster, a canary, one horse, but one child turned up with a rabbit and another with a ferret, so that made for a worrying morning, both animals eyeing each other keenly.

On nature walks, we'd always head up the Ystradfellte Road and, just before we got to the open common, there was a house where a horse would answer the telephone. The front door was always open in summer and, if the telephone rang, this horse would take it upon itself to amble from the small front paddock, into the house and lift the receiver off the hook. Nature in all its wonder.

Next door to the school, there was the Forester's House. Relationships between the local farmers and the Forestry Commission were, generally, good but not always. I was once told by the Forester that he'd received a mysterious phone call, stating "There's a fire in the forest." "Where?" he asked. "It's starting tomorrow," was the reply.

It's sad to report that both Ystradfellte School and Ysgol Thomas Stephens, Pontneddfechan, have now closed because of lack of numbers. Seven years of a man's happy experiences plucked from the archives.

THERE'S SOMETHING IN THE GROUND, A LEY LINE OR A LINK WITH THE ANCIENTS

Carreg Cennen Castle is a kind of pilgrimage centre

for me. As I described earlier, I don't know why, but once a year, when I was young, children of neighbouring villages, especially those in the Amman Valley and beyond, would walk to Carreg Cennen Castle on what was Whit Monday, the old Bank Holiday at that time of the year. It was not unusual to have a hundred or more children there from the various villages, all arriving with their ex-army haversacks, containing their bottles of dandelion and burdock pop, or water and all kinds of sandwiches, including my favourite, condensed milk – lovely.

Fun and games would be indulged in during the day and all kinds of derring-do down in the dungeon.

In the evening, everyone would make the long trek back to their various homes. My route was over the Black Mountain.

In later years Carreg Cennen became courting country for me, because I had been told, by a soothsayer of the area, that there's a certain romantic power about the place. If a girl cannot succumb to your charms in Carreg Cennen Castle, she never will, and the relationship was never meant to be. I confess to having tried out the potent force of the place myself – successfully too.

CLANDESTINE COFFIN ON THE EPYNT

I have skirted the Epynt Mountain on countless occasions, travelling through Pwllgloyw, Lower Chapel, Upper Chapel and on to Builth Wells, dipping down past the Griffin Pub, now a private house, which was famous for late-night drinking by SAS members in wild moorland training, and for a poltergeist that threw ornaments around, even in the cold light of day.

Sometimes, I turned left after Upper Chapel, taking the road to Garth and Llanwrtyd Wells. This route takes you across the British Army practice ranges and you pass through the austere "village", built for anti-insurgent and anti-terrorist exercises. On the hill, with the wide, wondrous views stretching northwards, beyond stands the lonely Drovers Inn, ghostly and stark, doors permanently shut to any weary traveller.

It was closed many years ago, at the time the whole area was cleared of its population when the army took over the mountain for training and the sake of the nation. There are a couple of signs on the Epynt, warning you,

IF THE RED FLAG IS FLYING, DON'T USE THIS ROAD

The red flag is always flying, tattered on the edges, but flying.

I have often been regaled by Dr Elwyn Bowen, of Cefn Coed, now sadly deceased, who knew more about the Brecknock region than any man I've known. The Epynt was a place that provided a perfect back-drop to the exciting tales of clandestine journeys across the mountain. It is said, by those who know, that during World War II, a hearse was seen being driven over the Epynt each day. It wasn't that the death rate way above average in the area; the coffin in the hearse had no room for a body, because it was stuffed with butter, eggs and bacon, destined for the black market in Brecon and the south.

Elwyn, who was the headteacher of Beulah School at the time, was, himself, caught, as he rode his motor-bike back to Cefn Coed one weekend. A policeman flagged him down and found a salmon, courtesy of a poacher, tied around his waist. Fast talking got him off.

"DOWN THE FALLS" IN GCG

Gwaun Cae Gurwen, or the "Waun" as we knew it, was a great attraction on a Saturday night. It had a cinema where you could do your courting just outside your own village and, if you weren't successful, fewer people knew, so it didn't matter. After the early show on a Saturday night, you also had time, before the last bus home, to continue your courting, down by the viaduct, or "down the falls" as it was known, because the river had a small cataract and sharp fall of water.

The viaduct was unique. It was built to carry a railway line, but the line was never built. I remember as a little boy crossing it with my family to visit an aunty who lived on the Gwrhyd Mountain on the other side of the valley. Looking down at the river far below made me giddy.

Under the viaduct was a very popular courting spot, you had to go early to get a place.

Gwaun Cae Gurwen Common, which stretched to Tairgwaith, gave me experience of the "monkey parade" of by-gone days, where the boys would walk on one side of the road and the girls the other. Looking across the road and "fancying" was one thing, actually making a move and crossing over, quite another. You looked a right berk if you'd misread the signs and ended up trailing back with your tail between your legs.

That was the era of my shiny green trench coat. God, it was magnificent, leather buttons and buckles everywhere. It was a bit big, but it didn't matter, it was the only trench coat in the valley and it distracted attention from facial teenage spots. It took me that extra mile away from duffle coats, which were very much in vogue at the time. There were hundreds of duffle coats walking the common, but my trench coat was a conversation and traffic stopper.

A LOVE AFFAIR WITH LIMESTONE

Llangattock Ridge is a dramatic limestone escarpment overlooking the beautiful Usk Valley above the village of Llangattock and the town of Crickhowell. I was, happily and luckily, headteacher of Llangattock School for four years.

It's an extraordinary thing that I have spent most of my life on, or near, limestone. Overlooking Brynaman, my home village, a limestone ridge forms part of the Black Mountain, the western reaches of the Carmarthen Vans and the Brecon Beacons. The carboniferous limestone – you can tell my geography training is coming out now, stretches eastwards through Pontneddfechan, on limestone, where I was headteacher for seven marvellous years and on to Penderyn, on limestone, where Richard, our son lives, and where I often chose to drink at the old Red Lion on the old drovers road from Neath to Brecon.

On many a morning as I drove to work in Llangattock, I would come over the limestone ridge from Garnlydan and Beaufort, to look down on a vast expanse of thick white clouds, lapping the lower edges of the Usk Valley. No town or village could be seen, but each hill and mountain were islands standing above the serene, flat -topped, silent lake.

Not so quiet were other journeys. I was late leaving Llangattock School one evening because of a governors meeting and, as I drove up from the village towards Beaufort, I came across an extraordinary sight. The Falklands War was at its height then, and up on the ridge, in the fast-dropping dusk, a night war-game was going on between two forces of Ghurkha troops.

Jeeps with coloured flags carried umpires who had the last word as to who was "dead" or "injured". Helicopters without lights hovered above the slopes and moorland, dropping more troops. I have to say that, had I been captured and, knowing myself as I do, I would have told them everything that they wanted to know. As it was, the scene became even more surreal, when an officer with a brightly coloured arm-band held his hand up to stop a jeep driving through the melee, and waved me through.

LAY-BYS IN MY LIFE

GET TO THE BACK IN BARRY

FOR THE ANNUAL VILLAGE trips, club or chapel, Barry had the edge over Porthcawl for me, because it was further. The buses or coaches would park in what seemed to me to be a line of garages around the headland of Nell's Point, where Billy Butlin built his holiday camp. Now all gone, of course.

Barry Island was sand, sea, candyfloss and toffee apples, with an hour in the fair before we went back on the bus. On the journey home there was always a collection for the driver, a cap being passed around, and a singsong all the way home,

"She'll be coming 'round the mountain as she comes, Singing aye, aye, yippee, yippee aye, She'll be coming round the mountain, etc. etc. ..."

It was a great rendering, if not entirely eisteddfodic, certainly enthusiastic. There weren't any hills on the way home, but we were "coming round the mountain" for mile after mile.

BREAKING A RECORD IN CAIO

My great-grandmother gave birth to my grandmother when she was just twelve years old. Genealogy is fashionable these days so, I've been at it too, and that piece of information was thrown up in my searches. As was the custom in those days she was sent away from home to stay with relatives. In her case, a small cottage next to the rectory in Caio.

We don't know who the father of the child was, nor do we know anything of the father of my mother. The man I thought was her father and, my grandfather, was not, on investigation, so there appears to have been a run of this kind of thing in the family. Oddly, both my great-grandmother and my grandmother worked, for a while, as maids in big houses or estates in Llandeilo, Llanwrda and the Pumsaint area of Carmarthenshire.

So, who's to know – I could be an heir to a sizeable chunk of the eastern part of the county. Such aspirations, claims, and subsequent possessions, wouldn't change me at all. Of course.

Caio is a beautiful small village, just off the main road between Llanwrda and Lampeter. It's not far from Pumsaint and the Dolau Cothi goldmines. The family connection, on my mother's side, certainly goes back to there. I have ancestors buried in Caio and nearby Crygybar.

When I was a little boy, we often made family visits there. The family links were two great aunts, Aunty Marged and Aunty Hannah, sisters, who were as different as chalk and cheese. For some reason lost in their past they didn't speak to one another, but they were both married to men called Dafydd, so there was some common ground.

Aunty Hannah lived on a smallholding, halfway between the main road and Caio itself, and on our walk from the bus to the village, we called there for lunch. They were a lovely, welcoming couple and the house was always pristine and tidy. Uncle Dafydd kept bees, so the honey in the pots had only travelled 20 yards.

Aunty Marged was a different kettle of fish. A colourful character, she lived next door to the Brunant Arms, in Brunant Cottage. She was worldly-wise and interested in politics, both local and international, and was often seen standing at her door, catching gossip as it passed by. She was not interested in trivia or the day-to-day niceties and, it was common to find magazines behind the cushions of her settee dating back to the 1930s and 1940s. Although untidy and "come day, go day" in speed and attitude, she made a marvellous tea in the kitchen when we arrived. She backed up sandwiches and cake with tins; I didn't mind that, I loved tinned Ideal Milk on my red jelly.

On the way back from Aunty Marged's, we'd again call in on Aunty Hannah, before walking on to catch the bus. Her first question was always, 'How is she up there?'

Aunty Marged had also asked, when we arrived at Brunant Cottage, 'How is she down there?'

So there was concern, although they weren't speaking.

The downside of visiting Caio, in my early years, was the fact that the village was not on the mains sewerage system and in both houses it was a question of a bucket out the back. Now I was not of the gentry, but I was certainly not used to that.

Thunder boxes were not in my sphere of experience and I think I still hold the record, in Caio if not further afield, for not visiting "the little house on the prairie" for at least ten hours. It takes a lot of discipline and distraction to accomplish that.

My father, on the odd occasion he joined us on the Caio pilgrimage would always call in the Brunant Arms, next door to Aunty Marged's cottage. My father had a long fuse, but he nearly flipped one year on being charged one shilling and sixpence for a pint. It was only one and two pence in the Black Mountain Inn, Brynaman. Halfway through drinking the pint, in chatting, the landlord suddenly realised he was related to Marged next door.

'Oh,' he said, 'sorry about that, here's four pence back, I thought you were a tourist.'

STOP-OVER IN SENGHENYDD

Senghenydd is a name that reverberates in Welsh industrial history for all the wrong reasons. Twice, in the early years of the 20th Century, massive mining disasters blotted the memory of the working man. The second explosion, on October 14th 1913 saw a black record broken, when 439 men and boys were killed. Some families lost three from the same house. Compensation was greater for horses than for men, so the record of the establishment and of government has a permanent stain against the name – Senghenydd

I was introduced to the village, for the second

159

time, in January, 1972. It was a stop on my teaching trail and, for the two years and a term that I was there it was a happy and fulfilling interlude. The school was on the side of the valley and has long since closed; the children are now schooled in a new building on the very site of the Universal Colliery – the explosion mine. The school being there is a kind of determined gesture for the future, defying the deadly downfalls of the past.

Senghenydd is almost a dead-end valley but you can rise out of the village and take the mountain road over the moorland to Nelson, taking in fine views towards the valleys of the north.

It is a road that closes very quickly in the snows of winter, as Elaine and I can testify, for we travelled that route daily, me to Senghenydd, Elaine on to Abertridwr.

I played rugby for Senghenydd RFC some years before I went to work there. That was my first introduction to the Aber Valley. The team was struggling at the time and they had sent down to Cardiff Training College for any spare bodies. I was very spare: I wasn't required by any of the college teams. It was 1962, and here lies a confession that I'm pleased to get off my chest because, for playing at Senghenydd, I received 7s 6d "boot" – unofficial expenses. I played just twice and it was rumoured that they were prepared to offer me 10s 6d just to stay away. The clear message was "We're short of players, but we're not that desperate."

TAIRGWAITH AND THE TRAIL OF TEARS

Tairgwaith is a village, out on a limb, not far from Gwaun Cae Gurwen. It was set up to accommodate men who came from other areas to work in the coalmines of the area. Unlike most of the schools in the Amman Valley, where most of the children spoke Welsh, many of the children in Tairgwaith were English-speaking.

My father worked in the mines of the area, first in Steer Pit and then, beyond the village, in East Pit. It was also the village nearest to the place where my grandfather was killed. Francis Lewis, my grandfather, or the man I thought was my grandfather, died in Steer Pit following an accident.

I clearly remember the day his best friend, David John, came home to tell us of the accident. It was not unusual for a miner in dirty clothes to walk the roads in those days because there were no pit-head baths, but to come home between shifts, to a street in which he didn't live, was usually not good news.

I was ill in bed on the day that it happened. I was seven years old, suffering from measles. My mother was shaking the bedroom mat out of the upstairs window when she said, 'David John is coming, that's odd.'

David John was a great pal of my grandfather's in work and play and often stopped in my grandmother's house for tea, cheese and pickles after a night at the Black Mountain Inn. He didn't live in Chapel Street as we did and, as I looked out of the window, the sight of him walking along the street brought women to the doors of other houses.

When my mother opened the door to him, he said bluntly, 'Francis is dead.' – and that was it.

He was kinder when he went on to tell my grandmother. He mentioned an accident, things didn't look good but, you never knew, the hospitals could do wonders, one could only hope. Francis Lewis was dead. Mam and I knew.

Distressingly, and with an odd quirk of fate, another family member was lost on the road to Tairgwaith. My cousin Derek's son was killed by a car as he walked home with friends. He was a Noble, and his death means that our son Richard is the only male left of his generation to carry on the line.

OVER THE TOP AT TREFIL

Just to the north of the Yellow Brick Road – the A465 Heads of the Valleys Road – lies Trefil. You take a turn off the Tredegar roundabout, head for the Usk Valley and rural mid-Wales and you'll come across the small village. You will not get to either the Usk or the rolling hills of Wales's wide midriff, you'll end up, beyond the village, in a disused quarry, a place of late-night clandestine courtships, unofficial liaisons, fine views and a definite full stop. It's a dead-end.

I have spoken at the rugby club dinner there twice and, on each occasion, it was a convivial, vibrant and welcoming night. Who was that fellow who started his soup before grace by the way? The Chairman had him. Something similar to the Tonna

RFC experience, another fine bash, when the Chairman of their club, in mid conversation with me, said, "Excuse me a minute Roy."

Whereby he left the table, went over to the youth players' corner, grabbed one rowdy youngster by the lapels and, in his ear, quietly but firmly, suggested that his future at the club, and in regular breathing, were in jeopardy if he didn't behave himself. It was all sorted out with the Chairman's laser stare.

'Sorry Roy,' he said on his return. 'These youth players are the future of the club, but after four pints they think they're Tarzan. They've a low threshold of intoxication see. I worry for the youth of today I do. No resilience, mun.'

Trefil RFC could have featured in a "Gren" cartoon of Aberflyarf; for their pitch is on high ground with slopes that eat up rugby balls once they're kicked to touch. The club, in those days, had a wonderful means of conveyance – the Black and Red Devil. It was an ex-Blaenau Gwent day ambulance painted red and black – club colours – with the hydraulic hoist for wheelchairs still attached to the rear of the vehicle. It had 20-something seats so it was really a bus and was used regularly on weekends for team transport and for ferrying those "over the limit" back to their homes once "Time" was called. For those unable to climb the steps of the bus on such occasions, the hydraulic lift was a tremendous boost. They were merely placed on it and, for 50p, taken to their door.

PUFF, PUFF, DADDY JOHN

I never wanted to be an engine driver. I was always a bus man, because of my father's years working for the James bus company in Ammanford.

Next door to Gu's lived the Salters, a railway family. Les was a signalman and John, his oldest son, became an engine cleaner, then fireman, then driver.

Brynaman had two railway stations, the LMS line, leading to Swansea, via Cwmllynfell and Ystalyfera and the GWR line, leading to Ammanford and Llanelli. The trains only had two carriages and there were no corridors. Each compartment had sepia-coloured photographs of holiday places in far-flung resorts in England like Torquay, Harrogate, or Weymouth.

I once shared a compartment with John Cale, the cult musician of Velvet Underground fame, based in New York. He was in the grammar school in our year and lived in Garnant, between Ammanford and Brynaman. He was always a talented one-off, an eccentric before we knew of such animals. On that journey we shared, he was desperate for a toilet and as there was no corridor, he headed for the leather-belt controlling sliding window. I bet that stretch of track near Glanaman had rare buttercups and daisies that year.

A few images of train journeys from Brynaman have stayed with me. On a special trip to Swansea along Swansea Bay, as we passed the gaol, I saw an arm stretch out of one of the barred windows and shake a handkerchief in the wind. It struck me as sad at the time. It must have been a powerful subliminal message, for I've retained it ever since.

On the return journey, I was reduced to tears. I had sunburn and Megan Thomas tried to rub "calamine lotion" on me, roughly. Tender, don't talk.

The big railway event in my life was the combined school excursion in 1951. All the schools of the Amman Valley got together to hire a train for a planned trip to the Festival of Britain in London. Joy of travelling joys, the train had a corridor along its entire length. Such was the excitement and the leniency of teachers during this new experience, that many of us walked to London, back and forth along the corridor.

On the embankment in the great city, we were told to keep away from spivs; especially the ones selling plastic jumping beans, we were to save our pennies for the Festival itself.

I was so tight with my money; I had quite a bit of spare on Paddington Station, prior to the trip home. I just had to spend it. At the platform kiosk, I spent it all on a book, *The Canals of France*. To this day, I have never visited them.

YOU DON'T WANT TO GO ON HOLIDAY WITH THE NOBLES

"The Nobles are coming, Hurrah, Hurrah."

PUNCTURE IN PALMA

ELAINE AND I WERE the victims of the "flat tyre scam" in Majorca. On landing in Palma, we set off to the hire-car place, picked up the vehicle and drove off, only to find that, within a couple of miles, we had a flat tyre. A car came up alongside us on the fringes of the city, with three young men in it. They kept pointing at our tyre, opened their car windows and shouted, 'Puncture, puncture, you stop, we help you, we help you.'

Elaine said, 'I don't like the look of those, keep on going, flat tyre or not.'

So I kept on going and our escort car soon disappeared, with me wondering if a genuine offer of aid and assistance by three young locals had been thrown back in their faces. Eventually, we had to stop and I turned into a side road. Immediately afterwards, another car parked behind us and out of it came a very smartly dressed young man, blazer and slacks, with a very attractive young lady beside him, who offered to help us. He was as smooth as a time-share salesman on bonus, but very friendly. He helped me to remove some of my cases, away from where the spare wheel was situated, and while he was actually waiting with me and trying to help me replace the wheel, Elaine was chatting to his girlfriend. Then, he went to chat to Elaine, leaving me to struggle with the tyre. Unbeknown to us, this was a distraction, because his girlfriend must have crept on the traffic side of the car, which was quite dangerous, opened the passenger door quietly and stolen our hand luggage. By the time we realised what was going on, they had climbed back into their car and swiftly driven off.

We checked our cases and discovered that all the hand luggage had gone, in which were important documents, mobile phone, passports, credit cards, money, diaries, address book and insurance details. We were stuck. Eventually a gentleman, whom I thought was either a drunk or a tramp, came along, and fair play to him, he helped me to change the tyre. I tipped him from money I had in my pocket, and we set off back to the hire-car depot. They claimed no responsibility whatsoever, even though someone in their garage must have known which cars were going out. We then had to find the police in the airport, who were not much help at all. None of them spoke English; they just gave us a form to fill in, as if this was an ordinary, day-to-day, occurrence.

The following day we had to go to the Consulate in Palma, to get temporary passports, and it was like being in a crowded doctor's surgery, all the people who had been victims of various scams in Majorca that particular day, or weekend or week or whatever, were there. We were a "shared sympathy" motley gathering.

One couple, of advanced years, had come in by a flight the previous night. They had been met at the airport, driven to the correct hotel, on the correct coach. On arrival at the hotel, a smartly dressed young man met them in the foyer. He said, 'Ah, Mr and Mrs Davies, welcome to the hotel and welcome to Majorca. You are on the sixth floor, if you go to up to the desk and sign in, the porter will take your cases to your room and you will find them there. We are pleased you chose this hotel, we hope you enjoy your stay; do let us know if we can be of any extra service.'

They never saw their cases again. Actually the smartly dressed "blazer" man, who met them in the reception of the hotel, didn't work there at all. How he knew their names no one seemed to know.

We eventually received the temporary documents we required and enjoyed the rest of the holiday. On my return to Wales, I wrote an article in the Independent and also for the Mail on Sunday and we had responses from many places in England. Not only had other people had exactly the same thing happen to them, with the flat tyre scam, but they also described the very same cars that were involved in our incident. I wonder if the Palma police have responded to these reports?

NOT SO NICE IN NICE

Nice is a lovely seaside city, French, Mediterranean and sophisticated. Elaine and I spent a lovely few days there, but two incidents coloured the holiday;

one a matter of life's extended, funny, experiences; the other, a darker tone of discomfort.

On a hire car journey to San Tropez, we stopped at a roadside restaurant with magnificent sea views. It proved to be very French, I don't know why that should have surprised us in France, but we could not decipher anything on the menu. We took a chance and I opted for something that, vaguely, sounded like "steak" when you read it out loud from the menu. I should have known I was in trouble when the waiter took my knife and fork away and replaced them with cutlery that looked like medical instruments.

Elaine advised, 'Look, tell him you made a mistake, and he'll take it back.'

I said, 'No, no,' I was too proud to do that, so what I did was to order lots of bread and two or three pints of lager. When the shellfish came, I didn't recognise them at all. They certainly weren't cockles, they weren't mussels; they weren't oysters. I didn't know what they were.

Elaine said again, 'Leave them, will you. You know what you're like with shellfish; you'll be up in the night.'

I wouldn't admit defeat, so I doggedly followed a procedure – Shellfish, chunk of bread, lager – shellfish, bread, lager – shellfish, bread, lager. I was proud of myself and managed to clear my plate. I wasn't ill and, contrary to past violent and weakening reactions, I didn't have to get up in the night at all.

It was, truly, a wonderful stay in Nice, but the last night spoiled it. As we came out of the restaurant after our final meal, we came upon a road, which was entirely pedestrianised, with lots of restaurants and hundreds of people eating "al fresco". A tall black man, dressed like an Arab, immediately approached us. He asked, 'Excuse me, where you from?'

I answered, 'Wales.'

He said, 'Ah, Wales, is that part of Scandinavia?'

I said, 'No, it's in Britain.'

'Well,' he replied, 'on behalf of the French Tourist Board, I would like to give you, for your wife, a bracelet, as a thank you for coming to Nice and to France.'

'No, no thank you very much,' I protested. 'We've had a lovely week here in Nice, that's fine. No need for this kind gesture.'

'No, no, please take it, it won't cost you anything at all, it's just a gift.'

I refused again. 'No, it's very kind of you but we don't want it.'

Then the mood changed. 'You are not taking it from me because I am black.'

I answered, 'Not at all.' But by this time, his "honchos", two big men either side of him, had closed in on me as well.

He repeated, 'Take it, it's free, from the French Tourist Board.'

So, to end the confrontation, I said, 'All right, we will take it as a gesture, thank you very much.'

We went to walk away and he added, 'It's entirely free, but I have a wife and children at home, so if you can spare something from your pocket, it would be very much appreciated.'

I dug into my pocket and gave him a few coins, clearly not enough because he started, with the aid of his two compatriots, squeezing me up against the wall, and saying, menacingly, 'You have more than that in your pocket, look around, look around in your pockets.'

So I said to him. 'Look, I don't have any more in my pocket. In that restaurant, I paid for my meal with a plastic card.' On reflection, I shouldn't have said that, because he could have frogmarched me to the nearest bank's "hole in the wall". Thankfully, they looked around, saw many people looking at the unfolding scene, and decided to withdraw, leaving the bracelet with me, which I promptly, in my shakes, threw in a refuse bin.

It occurred to me afterwards that although there were hundreds of people about enjoying themselves in the open-air restaurants, or walking the brightly lit road, Elaine and I were entirely alone and, the threat was very real, very dangerous. No wonder that incident has stayed in the memory.

BOOTLEGGING IT TO CANADA

When Richard was quite young, we planned a trip to Canada. This was "Following in father's footsteps". My father had emigrated there when he was a young man, and we decided to follow his trail, seeing the places in which he lived and worked in the 1920s.

On the day of departure, I was working on my

programme for BBC Radio Wales; so Elaine and Richard came down to meet me. When we met up at the BBC, we had to open the boot of the car to get my case in. All went well, until Richard put the keys of the car on the case and then closed the boot. We were locked out of our own car and there was no way around it. When we called the experts from Volvo to come and have a look at it, they said, 'No problem, we will get to the boot via the back seat.' No chance. Through the back seat was easy, but, once in the boot, the cases were in the way and could not be removed. The keys were stuck in the boot and no master key was available until the following day. British Airways was not entirely convinced by our "we're stuck and we'll miss the flight" tale, and did not readily agree to replacement airline tickets for the following day at the same price. They finally "came good" just before their shop in Cardiff closed at 5.30 p.m., but it meant that all reservations and connecting flights had also to be changed.

The Volvo boot was invaded, successfully, on the following day and we got to Canada, 24 hours late. The thing about Canada is it's so big that everywhere is a day away. Well, for us, not only was everywhere a day away, everywhere on the entire tour was a day later as well.

HE LEFT HIS APPENDIX IN LAS VEGAS

Nevada gave us an introduction to the American medical system. We had been there for a few days enthralled and amazed by the hotels and the entertainment of Las Vegas, deep in desert country.

It happened at the Hoover dam. Richard felt unwell. He said he had a pain down the lower right side. We took him to the local medical centre, where he was given every test under the sun to cover all options. We were sent to the hospital where the diagnosis was appendicitis. The surgeon said, 'I think he has appendicitis but he seems to have had it very suddenly. It's up to you whether you want us to operate, or not, but if he was my son, I would have it done. It's not that I need the work ...'

Richard had the operation, which was successful, and they gave him a scar that really was "value for money" big. He couldn't be hooker for the Aberdare Boys Comprehensive School rugby side for a full season after that slice. It certainly wasn't a "key-hole" procedure.

The "value for money" aspect has stayed in my mind, for, as a West Walian, I understand the premise that you should only part with money under anaesthetic. It's too painful otherwise. All that happened in 1980, but I still remember the cost. The anaesthetist's fee was twelve hundred dollars, the surgeon's fee was eleven hundred dollars and the two-day hospital stay, plus drugs, came to 7000 dollars.

I wondered how some of the locals manage out there, especially the one-legged beggar I saw, who had a wooden sign around his neck, stating, "I will work for food."

ON THE CARPET IN GERMANY

We have dear German friends, Winfried and Inga. I first met Winfried many years ago on a Council of Europe Education Conference in the Black Forest. I even remember the conference title, "Education towards international understanding." I believe in that philosophy ... international understanding and, with Winfried's help, I was able to set up some exchanges on the Wales-Germany bridge.

We've always enjoyed our stays in Germany but on one occasion, involving a choir exchange between Baunatal, near Kassel, and Crickhowell, we couldn't stay with Winfried and Inga, so Elaine and I were billeted out to house of the chairman of the local choir and his wife. They were hospitable and courteous, but oddly, for Germans of that particular social class, they didn't speak much English. The wife's mother was the interpreter.

He was in charge of building houses for all the workers of the nearby Volkswagen factory, and he was very well organised, his own house being absolutely pristine; even his garage was extraordinarily neat. All the tools were lined up on the wall, according to height or length. All the pieces of wood that he had cut for the winter had the dates on which he had chopped them written on the end of each log.

On the first morning we were there, I was in the shower when Elaine, panic-stricken, rattled on the shower door, in tears.

'I have done something awful. I was just ironing something to wear today and without thinking, I put the iron down, on its end, on the carpet in the bedroom and it's left a brown burn mark. I went downstairs and I explained this to the lady of the house, a very gentle, lovely lady, who said, 'Don't worry,' in limited English. 'The carpet is very old, kaput; we will be throwing it out soon.'

So Elaine came down, feeling a little better about what had happened. I attempted to introduce a more relaxed atmosphere at breakfast. I started telling stories and leaned back on the breakfast table chair, at which the back of the chair flew off and shattered.

That evening they invited a few guests round to meet us. There was a clean, white tablecloth on the dining room table. After our meal, I gave him the gift we had brought. It was a working miner's lamp and, I had brought him oil as well so that he could light it. When I explained what and how it worked, our host said, 'I will put the oil in.'

I said, 'No, I will put the oil in. I know what to do.' I put the oil in the top, it shot out through the bottom and all over the white tablecloth.

They insisted, 'It doesn't matter, we have another tablecloth, this one is old.'

Elaine was distraught, but more was to come. The following morning, the car we had, a normally reliable Volvo, had poured about six or seven pints of oil all over his power-washed, red-bricked drive.

I would add that, the following year, he came over with their choir, and he stayed with us. He slept in our waterbed, but we forgot to turn it on, because the water needs to be warm. He made no complaint.

'Everything was fine, just fine,' he said. But had it been deep winter, he could have frozen to death!

CROCODILE TEARS IN VIRGINIA

Having mentioned the incident on our way to Canada, when we were locked out of the car, well … it happened again when we hired a vehicle in the eastern seaboard of America. I was indulging my weakness for visiting battlefields and we had already been to Gettysburg and Antietam, of American Civil War fame, and moved on to Williamsburg and Fredericksburg, famous conflict sites of the American War of Independence.

Taking a break in the tour, we visited a local country park, which was a wide-spread, swampy area, crocodiles included, as an added attraction. I stepped outside the car to take a few photographs. Elaine followed me when, for some reason, the car security system kicked in, leaving us outside the car and the keys inside. I tried everything to unlock it to no avail, so I decided to walk along the park road to seek help.

I found a warden's office and he immediately got in touch with a policeman, who came along in his car. A pristine gentleman, his trousers were so neatly pressed and seemed to have been sprayed on with a gun, you could almost see every muscle he had in his thighs, as Elaine pointed out to me. He tried everything, but couldn't get into the car either, so he telephoned a specialist car locksmith. The policeman left for other duties, having advised us that the crocodiles were "non-aggressive".

'Now you folks hear this,' he advised. 'If them crocs get inquisitive, or forget their manners, just climb onto the roof of the vehicle, and you'll be fine.'

Elaine and I spent the next hour all eyes and ears, our nerves bare on our sweating skin. The car locksmith chappie, eventually, came along, got into the car in three seconds flat and put out his hand for 50 dollars ... well, compared to a visit from the crocodiles, it was cheap, I thought.

A BIT OF BOTHER IN BOURNEMOUTH

Shortly after my father passed away, I decided it might be a good idea to take my mother and her brother, my Uncle Illtyd, for a short holiday to the south coast of England. We ended up in Bournemouth. We hadn't pre-booked anything, so we took pot luck and called at one of the hotels where there appeared to be a vacancy. It was a "Fawlty Towers" and then some. Gloom, doom and disarray were the three courses on the menu, no doubt about it.

Sitting, waiting for our evening meal, in a very full dining room, time moved into a different longitude and latitude. Waitresses finally appeared but, out of five of them, three were crying. It's a little disconcerting to have the delivery of your cream of asparagus soup accompanied by sobbing and sniffing. This went on for all three courses, putting me entirely off my apple crumble.

The following night, the same thing happened,

but, suddenly, the drama was heightened by sound effects ... there was an almighty crash of dishes from the kitchen, a door swung open and someone stormed out of the hotel, throwing off his white coat and putting his beret on as he went. The chef had abandoned us.

At breakfast on the following day, it was all put right. The waitresses were joy and "tar, la" personified and, a guest, from the north of England, in a broad accent, shot to his feet, and called for "three cheers" and a round of applause. We all complied. The next days were "four-star", except for the night of the frozen rice pudding, but at 25% off, who cared.

JUST PASSING THROUGH IN SAUNDERSFOOT

Away from home, I seem to be a magnet for the unusual incident or testing trauma. When working for BBC Wales in Pembrokeshire, I had a "visitation" in my hotel room.

I'd gone to bed fairly early on our first night and slept well. I woke at 5 a.m. and, thinking it too early to get up, I stretched over to check the alarm clock was still set for six. As I turned back to the pillow – there he was, a stranger walking straight past the foot of the bed. All I could think of saying was, 'Good morning.'

'Good Morning to you,' he replied, as he headed for the door.

I said, 'How the hell did you get into this room?'

He shrugged his shoulders and walked out.

Instead of jumping up and running after him, which was probably a good thing, as he might have been drugged up to his eyes, I shot around the room to see if he had stolen anything. I went into the bathroom and there it was: an open window. He had climbed up a fire escape, walked across a flat roof and then climbed into the room.

I have no idea how long he had been in the bathroom. It's possible he slept in the bath all night. I dressed very quickly and went downstairs. The night porter was at the reception desk.

'Excuse me; did you see somebody pass this way?' I asked.

'Yes, I did,' he replied. 'A gentleman who seemed very drunk or drugged, so I naturally assumed he worked for the BBC and called him a taxi.'

My jaw hit my slippers, I was speechless.

It turned out he was well known to the local gendarmerie, and they quickly apprehended him. That same morning, the hotel put "governor" latches on all windows ... you could open them, but the only thing that could pass through them was a slice of toast.

EXTRA TITBITS ON THE TRAVELOGUE

I could add the tale of the broken down speedboat on Lake Lucerne, with young Richard looking pensive, me tugging and re-tugging the engine starter wire, and Elaine shouting, 'Yoohoo ... help ... help!' at passing ferry boats.

Then, there was the pedalo with a rigid rudder

in Fuengirola. I slipped off the contraption, because we couldn't turn around and, we were heading for Tunisia. Young Richard, on board, was again looking pensive and apprehensive. I tried to struggle from the waves back into my seat. After half an hour I managed it, and a stroke of genius hit me ... we reversed back to the beach.

A Majorcan holiday had the added attraction of blasting in the site of the hotel being constructed next door to ours, with the resultant rock showers bombing our swimming pool. It must have been like that in Pompeii, when Vesuvius went ape.

Oh yes, what about the hotel in north Wales, with the bed on a 'two-step-up' plinth, and an unsafe-looking, heavy, chandelier above it. The room had a secret door halfway along the wide bookcase. I ventured through it, only to find myself in the public lounge ... in my pyjamas.

I could have mentioned all the above, but I won't; it would be too much. Holidays, or short breaks or "away days", with the Nobles, can be fraught. We appear to have a gift for the mishap or unnerving incident. I can't prove it, but I think that people who work at BBC Wales, friends and colleagues, make every excuse under the sun, diplomatically, mind, to keep their distance when I am on the staff list for an "overnighter". I can't blame them, because the occurrences are legion – and legend.

ONE LEG, THREE WIVES, FAIR PLAY TO THE MAN

IF YOU CLIMB THE Black Mountain by car, on the road between Brynaman and Llangadog, as you drop down the northern slope, the view before you is quite stupendous. Stop for an ice-cream there and take it all in. The small village of Gwynfe is part of the scene; as a family we visited Ysguborwen Farm there, which was kept by relatives.

Grand-uncle James Jones and his wife May lived there. She was his third wife. Wives seemed to come to the farm like "meals on wheels". James was a formidable character, a county councillor in Carmarthenshire, who had lost a leg in a threshing machine accident on the farm. He was also a genial man, and the fact that he'd lost his leg, made him doubly interesting, to me, it added to his esteem. If he'd have lost it on the Somme, it wouldn't have made him more of a hero in my eyes.

There must have been charisma there too, for his success with women was achieved with little effort. Fate served them up to him. His first wife became ill, so her cousin came to look after her. When she died, James married the cousin. In turn, she became ill and another cousin, May, came to be of service. The second wife died and May stepped up to the plate – well, up to the entire Welsh dresser actually. May saw him out, mind. In his case, "three times for a Welshman" was fatal – eventually.

A LONG AFTERNOON IN LAUGHARNE

Laugharne, beautiful Laugharne, is synonymous with Dylan Thomas but it goes back, way, way beyond Dylan to the time of the medieval knights when the Normans were in the area. Once a year, even now, the local inhabitants will beat the bounds, or walk the boundaries of the land they were given by the sitting tenant in Laugharne Castle so many centuries ago.

Laugharne, for me, though, is more present than past. No visit is complete without a tramp along Dylan's walk, to the famed Boat House, for a poetic uplift by the wild man's taped voice, a warm welcome from the ladies who work there and Welsh cakes and Bara Brith on the patio. Look out for two things: Dylan's ghost on the walk, for he has been seen, and the tide coming in on the estuary, like a mini Severn Bore, setting the waiting moored boats a-bobbing with anticipation.

So, to the Portreeve's breakfast – now there's an occasion. I was once invited as a guest speaker. It happens in October each year, when all the true men of Laugharne congregate for a salad breakfast and two speeches before embarking on a procession down to the Town Hall, for a quick prayer. Then, it's on to the church for a full service, back again to the Town Hall for another quick prayer and, at last, the thirst-quenching hostelries are hit, where no prisoners are taken and the drinking is at a pace to defy any risk of sudden dehydration.

Man, after all, lasts weeks longer without food than without drink. The men of Laugharne know this and their effective antidote for parched parts in the body beautiful eases the pressure on the National Health Service in the end.

WHAT'S UP DOC

Although Cardiff Castle is, mostly, a folly, it is a very convincing castle, built, as it is, on the base of a Roman fort, parts of which can still be seen today. It was a particularly impressive and desirable detached residence for the Normans too, as the Keep testifies.

I have a special regard for the Banqueting Hall, which is a magnificent room with a particularly attractive ornate wooden ceiling. It's marvellous for a wedding reception, but as a formal dinner venue I have found it to be a lucky place for me. I have spoken at many functions there with tolerable success. I particularly enjoyed a Cardiff Medical Society evening. I suggested in my speech that, for myself as a confirmed hypochondriac – having had three prolonged periods of that disease and enjoyed them all – it was a particularly safe place to be, if I had a "pull" as we say in Wales – a little heart tremor.

A surgeon quickly put me right.

'Listen,' he said, 'there are 120 doctors in here – that's about 100 different opinions, give or take 10 or 20.'

CLEANING UP AT ABERDARE RFC

Now here's an interesting tale. Aberdare RFC for many years was called Aberaman RFC. Donkeys years ago they were Aberdare RFC but were banned from the Welsh Rugby Union for paying their players. Subsequently, they moved two miles down the valley to Aberaman and continued playing under the new name. You could call them a club ahead of their time, because these days most clubs of the upper divisions are paying their players. I am a member of the club and I enjoy my visits there. On a Sunday morning there is a group of old-stagers who meet in the corner of the lounge bar and put the world to rights. The conversation is not always about rugby. It is about world events, local happenings and scandals. All human life is here and is dealt with under 'any other business' by the 'ad hoc' committee.

The club has a colourful chairman, Humphrey Evans, who is at present a District Representative of the Welsh Rugby Union and a lay preacher in the Unitarian Church. He can bury you, but he can't marry you – yet. You can't ignore him. He has a voice that could guide ships around Penarth Head … from Aberdare. During my days as a rugby referee, of very menial ability and low standing I have to say, he would often call upon my services, even after I had retired, saying that the booked referee had not turned up.

I was usually in charge of the 3rd XV, which was always a mixture of young boys who were keen and making their way upwards in the game and the more mature breed who were on their way down. They put their cigarettes out on the touch-line and had a quick cough before they took to the field.

Humphrey, at the time, was a local representative of Lever Brothers and my fee for the game was usually covered with a box of washing powder, courtesy of the firm. To be fair to him, he wasn't cheating Lever Brothers. All of the boxes of washing powder were damaged and were often given to me upside down, in case the contents fell out of the packet. "Cleaning up" in Aberdare was something entirely different in Humphrey's mind.

Aberdare Club serves rugby football well. Like so many other grass roots rugby clubs, they nurture the game, and turn out many teams, down to junior school level. The game, at this level, especially in the seconds or thirds teams is, sometimes, played with the right priority view of life. I remember standing on the touchline one Saturday when there was a skirmish and a ruck-and-maul nearby. As the opposing hooker bounced to his feet, he noticed me standing there and shouted out, 'Excuse me, Roy oh, on your programme in the morning, who's the mystery voice? That competition is driving me potty.'

You have to admire a man who, in the heat of battle, still has time to wonder about an intellectual challenge.

GEORGE BORROW B & B AT BRYNAMAN

Brynaman RFC is situated in the old Farmers' Arms in the village. It's a famous place. If you have read the book, 'Wild Wales' by George Borrow, you will know of this hostelry. In his travels through Wales in the mid-19th century, one misty night, Borrow came across the Black Mountain on his journey between Llandovery and Swansea and dropped down to an inn at Gwter Fawr, the original name for Brynaman. He entered the tavern and found men around the fire drinking jugs of ale. He, being a stranger, was viewed with suspicion and interest. They asked him if he had any news of the Crimean War, because they were off the main trail of solid news and juicy tittle-tattle.

Following his vittles and convivial chit chat, he retired to his bed. In the morning, there were men in the bar again, but they were a little more reticent and inquisitive about him, wondering if he was "checking them out" for some reason, so he thought it best to move on. There is now a plaque in the clubhouse which states "George Borrow slept here".

Some years ago, however, an historian turned up and suggested that George Borrow didn't, in fact, sleep in the pub at all, but spent the evening and night in a pub two or three hundred yards further up the road: The Brynaman Hotel – now closed. The club committee considered this news and opinion, looked again at the plaque on the wall, and unanimously stated, 'See that plaque on the wall? He slept here, right?'

So, officially, George Borrow "kipped" in the clubhouse, the old Farmers' Arms, right at the edge of the River Amman, which marks the county line between the old Glamorganshire and Carmarthenshire, dividing the village in two.

With local government re-organisation, Brynaman has been shifted and re-shifted twice over. Upper Brynaman has been in the counties of Carmarthenshire, Dyfed, and back again into Carmarthenshire.

Lower Brynaman, poor dab, has been rather more fluid in status, having been in Glamorganshire, West Glamorgan, Lliw Valley and Neath and Port Talbot. When I mentioned on air in my radio programme that, in giving out dedications, I was not as sure as in the past, where exactly, some villages were now situated, someone from the Bargoed area, wrote to me and said, 'You're quite right, Roy, I've lived in four counties and I haven't moved house at all.'

As for my playing prowess with Brynaman RFC, that is left in all its glory – subdued glory, in another chapter, entitled Sporting Icon … in my dreams – or should that be nightmares.

THE TICKET LARK AT THE ARMS PARK

Oh, how I could eulogise about the times that I've spent in Cardiff Arms Park and the lengths I could go to get a ticket. There's no challenge now, it's a totally different ball game, oval ball game at that. My acquired space, if lucky, was under the old North Stand where, however packed in you were, if liquid suddenly leaked from the grandstand above you around about half time, you still somehow managed to make space for whatever it was to hit the ground, just in case. Bottled or draft, you didn't want that falling on you.

Getting tickets, that was the thing. It was an art form, an initiative test. I built up a relationship with Bill Clement, the WRU Secretary at the time, and later Ray Williams, who also held the post. I started a correspondence with Bill, whereby I always sent him a begging letter, enclosing a stamped, addressed envelope and an open cheque made out to the Welsh Rugby Union. My ploy was that I was really asking on behalf of an uncle of mine for a ticket. This mythical relative had lost a leg at Dunkirk and an arm on D-Day, but he was a passionate follower of the game.

I did point out, as well, that if he was given a field ticket, when he got excited, he would tend to fall over. A grandstand ticket would be so much more comfortable for him and so much safer as well for a war hero and, as he was a gregarious man, two grandstand tickets would be even better, so I could, at least, tend to his needs.

Bill Clement never answered my letters but I always received the self-addressed envelope back, enclosing one grandstand ticket. What a wonderful man, recognising such dire need as he did. It was a game and he always played his part. For the following international match, I would send another note, stating,

Dear Mr Clement, I noticed that, when I sent the last open cheque, you extended the grandstand, I

trust it wasn't my contribution that allowed you to do that, but, if so, would it not be a nice gesture to name part of the grandstand after me – or my uncle?

Same response from Bill, no letter but, inside the stamped addressed envelope – another ticket. Ray Williams, as WRU Secretary, played the game too, for a while, but he was too canny and soon stopped. I think he checked up military records to find the man who lost a leg at Dunkirk but still managed to hop to the D-Day invasion, only to lose an arm for his efforts. Good job I didn't mention the eye he lost in the Dieppe Raid – that would have pushed it too far.

It was always one-upmanship, to be able to say that you knew someone, who knew someone, who knew someone on a committee – who might be able to get you a ticket. Now the distribution system and the hospitality occasions prior to the game have made it all a little banal and, dare I say, made some of the games, for a few punters, something akin to Henley, Wimbledon and Ascot. You don't really have to know what's going on, as long as you are there. Great shame.

YULETIDE AND THE CUSP OF THE YEAR

Go west to the Preseli Mountains and you can enjoy the New Year twice over. In the Gwaun Valley, they never changed from the Julian calendar to the Gregorian in 1752, so they still celebrate the Old New Year on January 13th.

Take in a pint at Bessie's, the Dyffryn Arms at

Pontfaen, while you're there. There is no bar, just a hatch for serving beer straight from the casks and you drink it in a time-warped throw-back to a small front room that welcomed its people in another century.

Christmastide in Chapel Street, Brynaman was a holly and cotton wool affair. As a small child, I never remember having a proper Christmas tree, fir trees didn't seem to be about then; the Forestry Commission, in our area, being just a twinkle in a forester's eye. We always had a holly bush with ideas above its station. In a good year it had berries on it and the seasonal snow was balls of cotton wool stuck to the window. Trimmings stretched across the room from each corner to the centre, with a big folding paper bell near the light, or just to the side of the light, because the bulb socket was our one household multi-plug, where wires stretched down if various electrical appliances were in use, like an electric fire. Toasters were not in vogue. Bread became toast when stuck on the end of a long fork and held against the fire. Smoothing irons were heavy, warmed on the coal fire, and then spat on to see if they were hot enough.

If our Christmas turkey was too big for the oven, it was taken to Francis the Bakers, to take its place in the queue for cooking. The bake-house ovens on Llandeilo Road were busy on Christmas Eve and Christmas Day in the years of the late 1940s.

Dad worked nights in those days, not in the colliery, but in the James's bus garage in

Ammanford. The buses ran on Christmas Day and he always rushed home to see if he'd beaten Santa, so that he could see the sparkly surprise on my face when I woke up. He never made it, for I was always an early riser. A 2 a.m. attempt postponed by Mam until 6 a.m. with, 'Shush, he hasn't been yet.'

I remember clearly the small electric train set Santa brought, not your normal Hornby Dublo ones for I was always, for years, too young to have one of those until, suddenly, one year, I was too old. My train set was a simple affair, with small fluffy brushes underneath the engine and carriages that sat on a vibrating, battery-driven track, shaking the train on its journey.

One of my earliest presents was a petrol tanker made of solid lead, deadly if you dropped it on your toe. Any brain inconsistency and inadequacy I have now, I put down to lead poisoning. There was always a pomegranate, a definite sign of Christmas in the shops, and a box of dates. The box label always had Arabs and camels alongside palm trees on the label and there were tokens inside that you collected to become a country member of the French Foreign Legion. I sent the tokens away and in return I got a plastic kepi with a neck protector against the Brynaman desert sun.

I always carried my presents to Gu's, my grandmother's, to show everyone what I'd had from Santa. It was there, one year, that I managed to stick a dried pea up my nose and got it stuck. Mrs Jones, next door, came in and turned me upside down, slapped me on the back and ordered me to blow. It came out on the third snort and although I was crying by then, I've never been put off peas soaked overnight in bicarb in a hairnet. The resultant mushy peas are so much tastier than the tinned, very green, peas.

Christmas Day was the one day of the year when beer was allowed in the house. My father would bring the flagons home from the Derlwyn Arms or the Black Mountain Inn and I was allowed a glass of shandy, little big man that I was. We once won a bottle of something sophisticated and sparkly in a raffle, but we kept that hidden in a cupboard under the big Bosh sink unit, behind the boot polish and brushes. Funny thing, sink units were often called "the Bosh" in those days. The word entered the language. Crockery went into the Bosh, washing went into the Bosh and, as a baby, I went into the Bosh for a bath. That's why one of my earliest memories is of a tap in the sky. My eyes would pinpoint it when Mam eased me back to wash my hair.

I never recall singing carols around the houses at Yuletide. There were only two occasions you could replenish your money-box. At weddings when all the children were allowed to put a rope across the road to stop the bride's car, until her father threw coins out, and on New Year's Day: the turn of the year was when the good god Janus, with his two heads looking both ways, was remembered at midnight by the St Catherine's Church bells and the hooters of the coal mines in Gwaun Cae Gurwen. At that point we were allowed out to sing on doorsteps and collect

Callenig.

"Blwyddyn Newydd Dda i chwi
Ac i bawb sydd yn y ty
Dyna yw fy nymuniad i
Blwyddyn Newydd Dda i chwi"

"A Happy New Year to you, and to all in the house, that is my wish, Happy New Year to you."

Traditionally, although you were allowed to sing at houses up until midday on January 1st, the real pickings were made from midnight to twelve thirty.

The Derlwyn Arms was favourite for the first "hit". There, the first singer would get half a crown, the rest mere pennies. Boys used to hide in the bushes and shadows from half past eleven on, keeping the Derlwyn in their sight of attack. And, at the first New Year bell or hoot from the Steer and East pits, we went "over the top".

I never made the half a crown. However strategic our plans, however well primed our position was for the off, out of some dark corner he came. Michael Lloyd, like an arrow. At the Derlwyn Arms' front door, you always ended up standing behind him. He was an SAS Commando before his time. He's driving coaches for Shearings now. I don't suppose many car drivers cut him up, there wouldn't be the space, nor the time.

FAGGOTS AND PEAS

When shopping, if my mother couldn't get anything she wanted in Swansea, the next port of call was Neath.

Neath has a lot going for it these days, as it did in the days of my youth. The N& C buses used to go from the "The Gardens" in Neath and my return to college on many a Sunday night was on the fast service, plush brown coaches of the N& C. There is one disturbing image that has remained in my mind and, it is not Neath's fault. It was there that I first really noticed shops with school uniforms in the windows. Other towns had similar shops but, when I think of school uniforms in shop windows, Neath fills my mind. If I saw them, it was always a depressing sign that the school summer holidays were coming to an end.

To balance that low was the high of Neath Market. My mother always made a bee-line for the market, because in the back were small cafés selling faggots and peas, followed by fresh, home-made apple tart and custard. Mam always regarded eating out as a priority when shopping. It was a break from the grind of having four men to cook for at home. If ever I go to Neath Market now, those early faggots and peas come back … I can smell them … and I can taste the tart.

KNOWING OUR PLACE

WHEN I THINK OF my mother and father, a feeling of inadequacy sometimes sweeps over me. At the end of their days, I didn't make enough of a fuss, I didn't rattle cages. I didn't fight their corner as well as I should have. It was in the blood I suppose, because Mam in particular, didn't like to make a fuss. Being the centre of attention was not her scene.

Even when I moved from being a headteacher to a radio presenter, I felt she was a little embarrassed and made uncertain by the fact that I was in the public eye. Secretly, I think she was quite proud of my progress but she liked to keep her counsel, expressing pleasure only when she could no longer contain herself, or when agreeing with someone who had already said what she might have, first.

I have nothing but warm memories of life in our house. My parents were very supportive and loving. My father was a convivial, gentle man. He had used up all the adventure within him when, as a nineteen-year-old, he had emigrated, with his cousins to Canada on a ten pound scheme. The journey took him from Liverpool on the SS *Montcalm*, to disembark at Quebec and then onwards for five days by train across Canada to

British Columbia.

Mam was a hard worker, the only woman in a household of four men, my father, Mam's two unmarried brothers, Thomas and Illtyd and myself. If the men were on different shifts, on their return from work she would sit at the table and eat "a little something" with them. Inevitably, this built her up over the years and she became quite comely. She was always bustling and busy. I made the mistake once of saying I was feeling a little down in spirits.

'Pull yourself together,' she'd scold. 'I haven't time to be depressed.'

My father, I was to learn later in life, had worked at many jobs. After returning from Canada, he'd been a painter, plasterer, butcher, collier and bus driver and conductor. In my very early years I only knew of him working for a bus company called James & Sons in Ammanford. He worked nights, cleaning and fuelling the buses and acting as relief driver and conductor if any of the crews did not report in for the early morning shift. I loved that time, because my father's bus-driving friends would indulge me by allowing me to sit on their laps as they drove the two bus stops from my grandmother's house to our house. Always in the dark of a late night, in case someone should see us and report them. It was a "sacking offence", but to be in the closed cab of a Guy Arab double-decker bus was a thrill beyond the norm for a six-year-old. Those days gave me a liking for and interest in buses, eventually culminating in the fulfilment of a lifelong ambition to hold a coach- and bus-driving licence myself.

I was twelve when my father announced he was returning to the coalmines. He'd had enough of night shifts and I remember my mother telling me his decision at the breakfast table. I felt sad at the loss of the bus connection, but also an inner pride that came with him having such a job. It meant more money and also the extra benefit of "concessionary coal", which was hugely important.

He worked at the Steer Pit and the East Pit in Gwaun Cae Gurwen. He was brought home from the pit one day, badly injured; a power supply pipe had exploded near where he worked. His head was swathed in bandages and, once the initial shock was over, I felt a swell of pride as to who he was, and what he was doing. Thankfully, he quickly recovered.

It was at the end of their days that I felt a little inadequate. As I said, Mam never liked to make a fuss. If she were ill, she wouldn't go to the doctor. She would only go there after she was better, to ask what she had been suffering from in the first place.

The good times lasted six years. Then pits began to close because imported oil was cheap. It was the late 50s and early 60s and Dad was the wrong age to be made redundant. No transfer to other pits was offered. He had moved a couple of years previously, to Abercrave Colliery, and this proved to be his last pit when Abercrave became victim of the cuts.

Money was tight and, looking back, I was of little help. I was in the sixth form of the grammar school and Mam asked me if I'd go on the "free meals" register. I refused, saying that I'd rather give up schooling and find work than go down a trail I considered embarrassing. Pathetic, even allowing for the supposedly sensitive teenage years and problems of self-image. My reaction makes me angry even now, when I think of it.

Being out of work, at the age of 60, was not the right time for my father to be idle. He wasn't ready for retirement. At the time the local council was renovating the old council houses, in one of which we lived, and workmen came daily to work on the improvements. My father was a very good plasterer himself and it would drive him up the wall, almost literally, if he felt the men weren't achieving a high enough standard. He had too much time on his hands. His inner tension though, was really down to the fact that he wasn't bringing a wage into the house. My uncles Illtyd and Thomas were bringing in money and Dad felt it keenly.

He was also a heavy smoker. He rolled his own cigarettes using Franklin Mild tobacco. They were, to be fair, the worst cigarettes I have ever seen in my life, because he simply didn't have the knack of rolling a good cigarette. They were skinny, wrinkly, pathetic-looking apologies for fags, but they suited him. The fact he was a heavy smoker and that he put on weight during his enforced early retirement, affected his health.

At night, lying in bed in Aberdare, I used to try mind exercises in "power transfer", whereby I'd visualize the road journey to Brynaman and try and carry my body strength or "wellness" to Dad, in an effort to make him better. It clearly didn't work.

The first cerebral thrombosis attack happened when he was 63 and it was then my feelings of inadequacy began to kick in. I remember Doctor Warner coming to the house on many occasions, once holding two fingers up at my father and asking him how many fingers he could see. We didn't really follow up with an in-depth medical investigation as I recall, and eventually, eighteen months later, my father had a coronary thrombosis and died in the house. He had been unwell for a few weeks and my mother was nervous that "something would happen" in the middle of the night, when she was alone. There weren't telephones in many houses then, certainly not in ours.

As it happened, Dad passed away during what the hospital called "social hours", dying in mid-conversation with Raymond Goss, painter and decorator, who was in our house, wallpapering, at the time. Raymond suddenly realised that my father hadn't said a word for a while. He turned around and Dad had quietly departed.

The loss hit me hard. I was working, as a teacher, in Senghenydd Primary School at the time and the bad news arrived mid-morning. I remember driving down the road, Elaine at my side, with the tears, slowly, flowing down my face, not crying loudly at all, but sobbing internally. I don't think Elaine had ever seen me cry until then. I did the rest of my crying on the mountain above my home as I walked towards Wimberry

Mountain, the place my mother had always warned me about. The place where little boys got kidnapped if they wandered too far.

At Dad's funeral, I remember thinking that he would have smiled at the chaos outside Morriston Crematorium. It was one cremation every twenty minutes in those days, with only one door for entry and exit, and our funeral was early. The funeral before us, a victim of a coalmine accident, was running late. There was a great mingling and milling of mourners, with some deciding to attend both funerals. The throng was such that it was like Tesco on a double points day. Dad would have chuckled at the unfolding scene of co-operative, chaotic grief. The funeral director asked me, at the door of the Crem, where I'd like the ashes spread – near the pine tree, or way over the main hedge. The thought occurred to me that, if they had been spreading ashes in this way for years, why weren't we knee deep in them. On reflection, I really should have arranged for Dad's ashes to be delivered to us, for burial, or for scattering on ground that meant something to him.

Even that arrangement is not without its problems. I recall a ceremony at Brynaman rugby field when the ashes of a club ex-player and stalwart were spread on the pitch. Prior to a game, one Saturday, the local vicar, together with family and close friends of the deceased, walked along the halfway line to the centre spot, had a brief ceremony and scattered the ashes. There was a stiff breeze and they spread widely. A wag in the crowd eased any embarrassment and discomfort, by quietly saying, 'Now, wasn't that typical of him as a player? Fair do, he always covered a lot of ground, didn't he.'

The days between a death and a funeral was an interlude I found a forbidding strain. Tradition decreed that, in the deceased's house, the curtains were closed and, out of solemn respect, all the neighbouring houses had their curtains drawn shut as well. It was a great lifting of the spirit, and the light, when the funeral ceremony was over and the mourners returned back to the house for "ham on plates". The atmosphere became, a perhaps forced, but welcome, easing of the dark, sombre tension of the previous three or four days. There was a relaxed mixing of funeral attendees.

Some families only met at weddings and funerals, so no one was quite sure who everyone was. I once heard of a man from Cwmgors who was a professional funeral attendee. Funerals were his passion and his pastime. He would check the "Western Mail" newspaper each day and tick off the convenient funerals he could attend. Back at the deceased's house, after the funeral, he was confident enough to stay for refreshments, because everyone there thought he was from "the other side" of the family. If anyone gently queried who he was, he would just say, 'Oh, we went back a long time. We were great friends in school.'

When ministers came to the house on the day of the funeral, it was their duty to give a service in the home and, if everyone in the house wasn't crying by the time the minister had finished his impassioned eulogy, then he hadn't done his job to best effect. Satisfaction for him was a great gnashing of hankies and a chorus of wails from around the front room. It was also common for a hymn to be sung outside the house and in those days many of the friends would walk in front of the hearse, while the family would travel in the car behind. This was in the days before crematoria, because a slow walk from Brynaman to Morriston would have taken several hours and entirely messed up the crematorium scheduling. So tight is the time-keeping that I have been in a funeral doing 45 mph in case they missed their slot.

We Nobles were never a close family. Like many families, we tended to meet only at weddings and funerals even though we all lived in the Amman Valley, with a spread of no more than eight miles between us. There was, also, a wee bit of a dilemma in the family, in that a couple of my father's brothers were not talking to one another. It went back to the time of my grandfather's death, Grandpa, my father's father from Pembrokeshire. There had been some problem over the will.

Each of the brothers and the one sister talked to my father, so we were on middle ground, the centre of family relationships. I remember, when one brother and his wife were in our kitchen expressing sympathy to my mother on the loss of Dad, there was a knock on the front door and when it became clear that it was another brother and his wife standing there, the first two went out through the back door to avoid any embarrassing confrontation or having to speak to each other.

My inability to help my father played on my

mind for many months and my spirits became quite low, so low that it triggered an incident some six months after his passing that helped ease my mind.

I had a vivid dream of visiting our home in Brynaman and, as I turned the corner in Mountain Road that led to the Derlwyn Arms and the house itself, I could see my father leaning on the gate, looking down the road towards me. As ever, he was smoking a wrinkly Franklin Mild cigarette, and was wearing his collarless, thick, woollen shirt. He waved to me and, as I got closer, he retreated back towards the house. By the time I got to the gate, he had reached the front door, where he turned, smiled warmly, gave another wave, went in, and closed the door behind him. At that moment, a great weight immediately lifted from my mind and a feeling of acceptance, even contentment, filled me. With my father, all was well.

Was it a dream, was it a safety trigger in my mind to allow me peace, or was it something more? I often wonder, even now.

My mother's passing was also traumatic and continues to feed a feeling within that I did not do enough for her. I would have put money on my mother lasting into her 80s but it wasn't to be, she died at the age of 69. The diagnosis at the time was Alzheimer's disease but I have never been convinced that was the correct diagnosis. At no time during her illness did my mother not recognise me. Certainly she had changed a little in character and when she came up to look after our son, when we were out, the reverse was usually the case, with Richard, at eleven years of age, taking care of her. When she left our house, to return to her home in Brynaman, she would always burst into tears, which was not her at all. Something was amiss.

I think it was something to do with her diabetes being out of control, but Alzheimer's was a fashionable and new word at the time and was very much used. My mother-in-law was also suffering from senile dementia, during the same period, and she had come to live with us. She certainly showed the classic symptoms of dementia, on occasions putting on three or four dresses, at 3 a.m., carrying three handbags and trying to leave the house to do some shopping. Although she had been a singer in operettas and musicals as a younger woman, she was a sensitive, quiet and private person. She would have been mortified at the things Elaine had to do for her in her later and last few days.

My mother was a bingo girl and she liked to go to the club for a drink with her friends. She was very lively and many of my friends, even now, remember her as sociable and always up for a chat. How she loved a chat. Her illness started when a car door swung in a high wind and hit her head. True to form, she wouldn't go to the doctor until she was better and then she went to ask the doctor what had been the problem.

From that period, various other things began to happen and she began to wander. She used to go with her brother, Thomas, to an agricultural show in Carmarthenshire and he found her roaming around the crowd one day after she'd been missing for a short while. After her death, I heard from friends that when she used to go to the bingo, she'd visit the toilet and be away for ages. Sometimes she'd be found, sitting in the foyer of the hall. Confusion, dementia – Alzheimer's, whatever causes the onset, it's a harrowing experience that drags carers and sufferers down into the darkening abyss of a character-changing long goodbye. I feel for all of them and I quietly support charities that offer aid and comfort to families under such a cosh of pressure and commitment.

I remember visiting Glanaman Hospital where my mother was a patient after her illness had taken hold. When I arrived she started crying which then graduated to deep sobbing. Nothing I did placated or eased her. She sobbed solidly for well over an hour. I also remember that in her last few days she was in a hospital in Llanelli when Elaine noticed a mark on her temple and reported it to the sister. The nursing sister said that she had been away for a few days and she had also noticed it, but we were not to tell anyone of her comments. In those days the hospital authorities ordered their staff not to discuss any incidents of injury to a patient that hadn't been noticed by the patient's relatives.

I was appalled at the way one doctor talked about my mother: as if she wasn't there. He would discuss her condition, across her bed, directly with me, reducing Mam to tears when she was in an entirely lucid state. There was a man who missed the "bedside manner course" entirely. A man devoid of all sensitivity.

I believe I have a longish fuse, slow to fire, but how I kept my hands off that medic's lapels I'll never know. To their eternal credit and with my thanks, most of the other staff, doctors, nurses, and auxiliaries were excellent ambassadors for their profession and tended my mother with professional, exemplary gentleness and respect. Dignity and respect ... everyone should have those expectations fulfilled, it's a measure of a caring, mature society.

During another visit to my mother, I couldn't find her. She was not in her bed or in the Day Room. Then I noticed a pile of what I took to be clothing, next to a settee near the window. It was my mother. I picked her up. No one else had noticed that she had fallen off the chair. I walked her quietly back to her room. For some reason, she couldn't pass any window without wanting to clean it, so the confusion in the mind was still there.

Finally the nursing sister said, 'Yes, I think there's definitely a mark on your mother's forehead, something has happened. We should check it out with an X-Ray.'

They took my mother to X-Ray – she had a heart attack and died on the table.

If the onset of Alzheimer's, with its awful trials, was becoming, at that time, generally better known, then probably my mother's sudden passing was a blessed release. However, I am still filled with doubt. At no time did she not recognize me. Was it Alzheimer's, or was it something entirely treatable? Had I reacted in a more aggressive and pro-active way, could I have made a difference? That question remains on the table.

THOUGHTS FOR THE MELANCHOLY MOMENTS

Inevitably, in the course of time, close family members and good friends pass on. Elaine and I often reflect on the losses and those who left a mark and memory on our minds. In each one of us there remains the essence and influence of those we once knew and were a part of our lives. In many cases we were fortunate to have known them over so many years, but there are the sad frustrations too.

My mother died far too early, so did my mother-in-law. Mam died on Elaine's birthday, Elaine's mother passed away on a Christmas Eve. Elaine's father on All Fools Day, April 1st and my father on July 4th, American Independence day. Other celebrations are fixed on days that are poignant in our family.

Special regrets centre on our son, Richard. Both his grandfathers died before he was born and he was only twelve when he lost both his grandmothers. In the years following their loss, Richard played the cello for Mid Glamorgan Youth Orchestra and there were occasions when the orchestra played in St David's Hall in Cardiff. Both his grandmothers would have been so proud of him had they been able to see him there. Elaine and I both are, secretly, jealous of friends whose parents are still alive, fit and well at the age of deep 80s, maybe edging towards the 90s. It is something that we have missed dreadfully in our lives. It would have been so nice to share our lives with our parents in the years when Richard was maturing and I was managing, quietly, to make a career in broadcasting. Actually, come to think of it, Dad never even saw me become a headteacher of a school. He would have been so chuffed at that, even more than broadcasting, because he always felt that you needed that solid, safe job behind you, not a "joking" one like the media.

EPILOGUE

And when I went to the County School
I worked in a shaft of light.
In the wood of the desk, I cut my name:
Dai for Dynamite

VERNON WATKINS, BORN OF Maesteg, hewn of Swansea and Bletchley Park, wartime National Codes and Cipher centre, wrote the above words in his work, *The Collier*.

Deep down, I suppose we all hope that, if we don't exactly leave a mark in life, we at least make a difference.

Having been influenced and sculpted ourselves by the people and events we encountered in life, we are now the sculptors; moulding and marking others, possibly without realising it. It's a responsibility when you think about it. As I said in the prologue to this book, never believe that your children or grandchildren don't listen to your opinion, advice, or anything you say; for thirty years or so down the trail, they will be saying things and doing things because they heard you say and do them. The sap will still flow and you will go on.

In this book, I have tried to weave a path through the forest of characters and around the corners of incidents that shaped what I am, who I am and where I'm from.

There are gaps of course. My work in the BBC is only touched upon here and there because of two reasons. One, this tale is primarily one of early and middle life. Two, I still work at the BBC, so the ground, although fruitful, could be sensitive, and in one or two cases heavily mined.

Nostalgia, as they say, is another land, fine to visit as long as you don't live there. I hope my excursions have been acceptable.

Youth has its vigour, naivety and enthusiasm, middle age its broth of dreaming, striving and experience and old age has its mystery. Well, it is a mystery to me because I refuse to accept it. Old age is always fifteen years further on, although I admit it has its "give away" signs, like a taste for bran flakes, the discomfort of a dripping tap. "Getting lucky" is finding a car-parking space near the door at the supermarket, and an "all nighter" is not going to the bathroom at all. When all of that hits me, I will report back to you. So far, I have the barricades against it firmly in place.

As my own person, I have definite beliefs, opinions and attitudes. Perhaps I should bring them out in a small red book, *Thoughts of the Noble Roy*.

Voting should be compulsory, even if you only spoil your paper with a comment. There, that's one. Working as a presenter at the BBC makes it very difficult to express them. In fact, it's a no-go area, so over the recent years I have made a virtue of avoiding commitment of view and thought. Show me a fence and I'll sit on it; I have the extra marks on my buttocks to prove it.

Even as a headteacher, I led by consensus, Japanese executive style. If there was a better idea from someone else on the staff, then so be it.

I'm not very good at confrontation, I do have a fuse, but it is a very long one and simmering is a slow process before I come to the boil. As you get older, there's more to life than a mighty clash.

That can be a problem in standing up for your rights, I suppose. The tale of the "moving hairy sultana" proves that.

At breakfast one morning, I was day-dreaming into my Swiss style muesli breakfast cereal when I noticed something.

'My sultana just moved,' I declared to Elaine.

'What do you mean, moved?' she queried. 'It's your milk just swishing about.'

I had one more mouthful when, 'There it is again, just there look.'

'Oh yes,' she agreed. It was dark brown like a sultana, about the size of my thumbnail in length, covered in hairs and was sharing my muesli.

I took it back to the supermarket, they sent it off to the supplier and a few weeks later, the findings came back, The creature had a long Latin name, had incubated in the muesli, probably in our cupboard, because we'd kept it too long, they said but, as a gesture of goodwill, they gave us a £2 voucher to spend in the supermarket. Health and Safety and legislation was not loose in the country then, so we let it go. £2, I ask you.

There are things that I've left out, my abiding interest in battlefields, for instance. Especially that critical moment in a conflict that not only decides the battle, but also the span of history itself. What would have happened if the Saxons had not got overly excited at the scent of victory at the Battle of Hastings? Would they have defeated the Normans? If so, not one stone would have been laid to build the famous large castles of Wales.

Would Wellington have won at Waterloo if Napoleon had not suffered from haemorrhoids? I wonder. Taking medication and a rest and staying off his horse probably made all the difference. Elaine, poor dab, has been dragged around many fields of battle, so that I can merely ponder that "what if" moment in history.

So who were the characters, and what were the events that sculpted the "life of Noble". Well, many have been listed in the book, but I could have included others.

Elaine Williams, a radio producer at BBC Wales, who died far too early, was a woman of culture and music. We worked well together, but her Irish experience sticks in my mind.

Broadcasting live from Cork, Elaine was having trouble with the Irish radio engineer in the studio. We had mistaken him for a cleaner, so things had not started well and, with just two minutes to go, there appeared to be no sign of us getting on air and broadcasting from across the sea to Wales and the world. Every capillary vein on Elaine's neck had burst and her skin was a quilt of red patches.

With 30 seconds to go, the correct switch was found, thrown and we were through and firing on all cylinders. Seeing Elaine's gasping, fraught state, our Irish host used a comment I've heard twice from an Irish broadcaster and it does put everything into priority context.

'Now, we do our level best here, but if we cock it up entirely, we have to remember, and give thanks, that it's only radio after all, we're not brain surgeons, so no bugger's dead at the end of it.'

True enough.

Thoughts of Ireland bring my mind to the much-loved, much-missed Ray Gravell; a warrior for Wales and the British Lions on the rugby pitch with a personality to fill an aircraft hangar and with a gift to lift you and make you feel the most important person in the room. An icon, hewn from the very rock of his beloved Mynydd-y-Garreg, he had an inner conviction that he was a reincarnated warrior follower of Owain Glyndwr, but a man with insecurities.

After a night on the "pop", while broadcasting together in Dublin, he telephoned me on the inter-room phone system at 3am with, 'Roy, it's Grav.'

'What do you want Grav, any problem?' I replied.

'Tell me now, what do you think of me really?' I could have told him quite clearly at that unearthly hour.

I paid his phone bill the following morning, for

he had no Irish Punts, a total of over £140. He had been on the telephone all night, to anyone who would talk to him.

As for his gift of making you feel "the one", I recall walking into a large room in Cardiff, packed with people, when a shout went up, 'Roy ow! Over here, I want you to meet someone.'

I walked over. 'Roy – meet Bill Beaumont, Army Officer, Captain of England, Captain of the British Lions. Bill, meet Roy – Brynaman Seconds.' It was said with the warmth and clarity that declared, "this is a level playing field, we are all equal, with different strengths, that's all!"

In Ireland, in the town of Listowel in County Kerry, I met two of the town's famous writers, John B Keane and Bryan McMahon. John's interview for BBC Wales's television was for a series I was filming on the "Celtic Corners of Europe". Bryan McMahon was a very different animal from John, who confessed to transgressing nine of the Ten Commandments. Bryan was a gentle ex-headmaster with a gift in two languages, Gaelic and English. He was of advanced years when I talked to him, but his way with words was still a wonder and, when I asked him if he ever suffered writer's block at all, he replied, 'Ah, Roy, I'm in my eighties now and my brain is not as fruitful as it used to be, so, if I want fresh ideas, I have to go grazing in the front lawns of other people's minds.'

In my broadcasting years I have been fortunate to meet so many people and visited many places.

There are staff at the BBC I would mention in legions for their valued friendship and guidance, but the list, knowing my luck, would miss one out, so let my accolades be all encompassing. My seven happy years broadcasting in Welsh for Agenda – now Tinopolis – on "HENO" a daily magazine programme was real cream on my trifle. So many names, like Ena the Friday-night cook, made it a grand interlude in my life. The programme was not without its critics because of its deliberate emphasis on "populist" Welsh. But I found it all very fulfilling. Working with Caryl Parry Jones and Dewi "Pws" Morris on a Welsh-language comedy drama was an added fillip. I was "Eric", the yob neighbour and I fitted the part uncomfortably well. So said very many friends, on the sharp side and from the customer side too – the viewers and listeners.

I must say that those in the limelight, the true stars, have been genuine people in the vast majority of cases. For a while I wondered about the possibility of being a guru or a talisman, for quite a few performers came into my programme at early stages in their lives and then fired off to the cosmos in their eventual attainment. Charlotte Church was one I interviewed when she was very young and Catherine Zeta Jones tried to teach me tap dancing on a Sunday morning programme, and now look at her. I've met both since and they still have their feet on the ground, as does Katharine Jenkins, whom I've known from the early days, and Barbara Dixon, Elaine Paige, Bryn Terfel, Jason Howard: so many.

One from the bygone days who impressed me immensely was Richard Todd of *Dambusters* fame.

He was an absolute gentleman. I was also very surprised about the frailties of well-known names, many of whom, on the conclusion of a radio chat, would always ask, 'Was that all right?'

I really should mention friends who are presenters of the same vintage, starting at the BBC, or in broadcasting, around about the same time. Frank Hennessy, a warm mixed Celt of Cork and Cardiff pedigree and a fine folk singer and composer. The irrepressible Owen Money, comedian, singer, with an ever-open generous pocket and a body that disregards his brain's directives on one or two of the extra-curricular areas of life's course. Dewi Griffiths, ex-outside broadcast television director, who now has a wonderful Sunday morning programme evoking the nostalgic music spanning the years prior to the mid fifties and, of course, Chris Needs, a "one-off" multi-skilled performer who has tapped into a niche audience who regard him as a late-night friend, confidante and therapist.

Mal Pope, what a talent, who was writing songs for Elton John and Cliff Richard when he was a teenager and now writes musicals. The door will open for him one day and it will have to be a barn door when the "recognition flare" is lit.

Producers, directors, researchers and managers too, a formidable list that helped smooth the road for Noble. Of course, there were other facets of broadcasting, the intrigue, the tittle-tattle, the vagaries of policy and direction, even a secret meeting in a quiet hotel away from the "Taf Mahal" BBC HQ in Wales. Those tales, as I indicated in the

"Prologue" are for another time, another place, perhaps another book. I have been a fortunate man and the BBC has provided, benignly in most part, my happy field of operation.

"A man's a man for all that!" So said Robbie Burns, and all "that" has been great for me. This book has concentrated on the early years, and touched upon the later stages and careers, the moulding and making of Noble if you like.

We're back to the future again, as mentioned in the Prologue, but in a slightly different way.

'Before you can have the foresight to see what's possible, you have to have insight to assess where you are and the hindsight to appreciate who you are, what you've done, and where you're truly from.'

If the gypsy's premonition comes true, I wonder, I truly wonder, what the third career will be?

Accent Press Ltd

Write a review and win a prize!

Please visit our website
www.accentpress.co.uk
for our latest title information,
to write reviews and
leave feedback.

We'd love to hear from you!